COLLECTING
Autographs

COLLECTING

Autographs

SUSAN BREWER

REMEMBER WHEN

First published in Great Britain in 2010 by
REMEMBER WHEN
An imprint of
Pen & Sword Books Ltd
47 Church Street
Barnsley
South Yorkshire
S70 2AS

ISBN 978 1 84468 070 2

A CIP catalogue record for this book is
available from the British Library

Typeset in Palatino
by CHIC MEDIA

Printed and bound in India by
Replika Press Pvt. Ltd.

Pen & Sword Books Ltd incorporates the imprints of
Pen & Sword Aviation, Pen & Sword Maritime,
Pen & Sword Military, Wharncliffe Local History, Pen & Sword Select,
Pen & Sword Military Classics, Leo Cooper, Remember When,
Seaforth Publishing and Frontline Publishing

For a complete list of Pen & Sword titles please contact
PEN & SWORD BOOKS LIMITED
47 Church Street, Barnsley, South Yorkshire, S70 2AS, England
E-mail: enquiries@pen-and-sword.co.uk
Website: www.pen-and-sword.co.uk

Contents

Introduction

W E'VE ALL HAD to sign our name at some point or another and, famous or not, most of us have signed an autograph book. Although they are not so popular as they once were, some children still take them to school to gather their friends' signatures, and they also thrust them at relatives and neighbours. The traditional book is small to fit easily into a pocket, and often has a leatherette-look cover with 'Autographs' written upon it, to ensure you know what the book is for. Inside, the blank pages are usually pastel colours – pink, lemon, blue, green, gold, cream and lilac – all enticing pages which make you want to write something special.

As children, we tend to scrawl our names and a sentiment such as the ubiquitous 'By hook or by crook, I'll be first in the book' or maybe, 'Don't kiss at the garden gate, Love is blind but neighbours ain't'. However, as we mature we realise what a great responsibility we undertake when we sign an autograph book. What should we put? Do we come up with a thoughtful entry in the hope it will guide the book's owner through life's rocky highway, or do we opt for something witty to demonstrate our sense of humour? Many people rely on quotations, especially from the greats, such as William Shakespeare, Robert Browning or Robert Louis Stevenson, while others remember limericks, funny rhymes or doodles, often from their schooldays.

Today, it seems that the traditional autograph book full of thoughtful entries is out of fashion. Nowadays an owner is more likely to get a rude, or even obscene, graffiti scrawl than they are to get a witty rhyme. Modern autograph books tend to be used in the pursuit of the famous, or even the 'Z-list' so-called celebrities who have enjoyed ten minutes of fame on a reality show. Later, the signatures will often be offered on the internet to the highest bidder, rather than be treasured through the years as were the albums from the early twentieth century and before. In this modern, media-obsessed age, celebrity autograph collecting is booming, with some iconic autographs selling for thousands of pounds. Another popular theme enjoyed by adult collectors is that of collecting historical autographs. Imagine the sense of wonder as you hold a document signed by some great man whose invention changed the course of history, or whose novels are classics we read at school and see dramatised at the cinema. Or that of a monarch whose colourful exploits still make us chuckle, or a military figure who commanded a great battle.

I confess I particularly love the old autograph books, dating from a more unsophisticated age when people had time to write in a clear hand, dream up a sentimental piece of prose or to paint a delicate picture. Some of these early books were enchanting, packed with thoughtful rhymes, witty sayings and watercolour paintings that must have taken hours to produce. The artistic talent of the Victorians and Edwardians – in fact of all folk right up to the 1930s – seemed to be of an exceptionally high standard and these earlier books are liberally dotted with paintings and drawings of landscapes, people, still lives, animals and flowers. Cartoons flourish in these books too. Those Victorians had a wicked sense of humour!

Maybe one day the autograph album tradition will be revived, and once again we will be busy writing, painting or drawing in each other's books to provide a lasting memento of friendship. Hopefully, if that happens you will gain inspiration from the entries in this book. Never again will you have to ponder 'now, what on earth should I write?'!

Susan Brewer

CHAPTER ONE

Why and when did people start collecting autographs

THE FIRST WORD a child learns to write is invariably their name. Long before they are capable of wielding a pen they will learn to recognise at least the first letter of their name, proudly pointing it out when they see it printed on signs in the supermarket or as labels on food packets. As soon as they make that very first attempt to write their name in wobbly letters, they will be performing an action which, in the course of their lives they will carry out over and over again. Just think how often we sign our name – letters, official documents, visitors' books, registers, bank transactions, petitions and certificates. It's an important part of our lives. Centuries ago many of our ancestors couldn't read or

write (right up until the late 1800s some people signed their name with their mark, usually an X). Family historians frequently find certificates signed with a cross and next to it the registrar will have written the person's name and the comment 'his (or her) mark'. Interestingly, with regard to family history, the 1911 census is the first to show the actual forms filled out by the residents as opposed to an enumerator and it is an amazing feeling to see the actual signature of an ancestor of a hundred years ago. It brings him back to life so much more than does a printed name as it's something he wrote with his own hand and we connect with that. Nowadays though illiteracy is unfortunately still common, most people can at least write their name.

There are two main categories into which autograph collectors fall. The first group collect famous signatures – maybe those of celebrities, historical figures or sports people – while the other category consists of the social collectors. Social collecting is the accumulation of signatures of friends and family, usually in a designated book. Often, keen collectors purchase books full of strangers' autographs too, because at one time writing an entry in an autograph book was an art form. Some older autograph books are stunning, filled not just with signatures but with verses, proverbs, scraps, sketches or beautiful paintings. Sadly, this form of entertainment has long been left behind. If you give a young person an autograph book today, it's likely that much of it will be filled with graffiti and rude rhymes by their friends. People have different attitudes nowadays, often wanting to outrage or shock rather than to pass on an amusing rhyme or gentle homily.

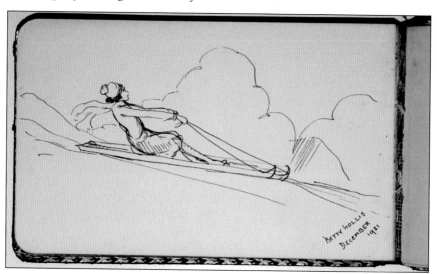

Collection of signed Star Wars ephemera.

So, how do you go about autograph collecting? The easiest way is to purchase an autograph album, or friendship book as they are often called, and to ask all your friends to sign their names and to add a comment or verse. Sometimes friends will stick photos inside which adds an interesting element and are perfect for reawakening memories years later. Often, signature books are made for a special occasion. When I married I passed around a book for the guests to sign during the wedding reception and planned a similar thing for my parents' golden wedding anniversary celebration. These books made treasured mementoes. Some people have a visitors' book which they ask their guests to sign, and maybe, to add a comment. This is a lovely way of recording your guests, as long as they aren't cheeky and don't write such things as 'The dinner was bland and undercooked' or 'Noticed lots of dust on the bookcase!' Visitors' books are also often found at places of interest and various attractions, and I always make a point of filling them in, because how often nowadays do you get to write your name in a proper album?

There are not many collectables you can get 'for free'. People say that nothing is free nowadays, but it is if you are prepared to wait around outside a venue such as theatre, where you know celebrities are performing. The traditional way of collecting autographs is to take your book and wait for actors and other celebrities at stage doors or recording studios. From end-of-pier shows, circuses, film premiers, book signings and stage door appearances to concert performances, there will be people who have tasted a bit of stardom and, equally, autograph hunters who want their signatures.

If you don't fancy the wait, then, for the price of a few postage stamps it is still possible to build a good collection of contemporary autographs. All you need to do, like so many other people, is write to some famous people in the field in which you've decided to specialise, whether celebrity, artist, politician or sportsman, in the hope of receiving a signed letter or photo. If you ask an interesting question at the same time and they answer it, that autograph and letter will be far more valuable and collectable than just a scrap of paper bearing a signature. The main drawback with writing is that you can't be sure if the celebrity actually signed the photo or wrote the letter himself as most celebrities have agents, assistants, managers, fan club secretaries or helpful family and friends who might well take over this task. At least if you go to see the star in person, you can watch him sign the book, and there will be no doubt of the autograph's authenticity. However, if you do need to resort to the post, at least there is the possibility that you will end up with a photo (though it does vary with the star). If he isn't too famous, and therefore not too busy – or too swollen headed – to write a note, you may well end up with a personal letter as well. See if you can forecast which autographs collectors will seek in a couple of decades' time. You never know, you might even hit the jackpot. (See Chapter 7.)

The heyday of the autograph album was probably the late 1800s and continued up to the beginning of the Second World War. It's from this era that so many of the thoughtful poems, pictures and elaborate inscriptions are found. During the 1950s and 1960s autograph albums tended to contain more lightweight rhymes or doodles, and a couple of decades later the books seemed to be used more for the collection of celebrity signatures than for those of friends.

History

Correctly speaking, an 'autograph' is a document written by the author in his own handwriting, as opposed to one typed, printed or transcribed, and you will find that many dealers and auction houses will use the term 'autograph document'. Nowadays, the term tends to be used for a person's signature, especially those of celebrities. The hobby of collecting autographs is known as philography, and so a collector of autographs is a philographist. Most enthusiasts though prefer to call themselves 'autograph collectors'.

The pastime of collecting autographs is believed by researchers to have started in the sixteenth century, when travel became more widespread. Before then few people would visit other lands, or even distant towns, but as communications opened up people felt the urge to explore. It is known that some German travellers kept albums of correspondence as they journeyed, and this practice became more widespread. There was also a trend amongst some European graduating university students to have their personal bibles signed by classmates and university mentors, and the signatures sometimes included small sketches or poetry.

Some publishers put blank pages into bibles and other books, purely for the purpose of accumulating signatures and snippets of information. It seems the first true autograph books, or 'friendship books' appeared in Germany and the Netherlands in the mid-sixteenth century. The oldest known is that belonging to a gentleman called Claude de Senarclens, a colleague of John Calvin, and dating from 1545. The friendship books were common in Germany with students during the following decades. Often these earlier books tended to be collections of ideas and beliefs, a kind of memorandum as opposed to a social collection, and frequently were small printed books containing woodcut illustrations. Another very early album dates from 1548 and is a copy of the *Loci communes theologici* by the reformer Philipp Melanchthon, and which was owned by Christopher von Teuffenbach. Philipp Melanchthon explained: 'These little books certainly have their uses: above all they remind the owners of people, and at the same time bring to mind the wise teaching which has been inscribed in them, and they serve as a reminder to the younger students to be industrious in order that the professor may inscribe some kind and commendatory words on parting so that they may always prove themselves brave and virtuous during the remainder of their lives, inspired, even if only through the names of good men, to follow their example. At the same time the inscription itself teaches knowledge of the character of the contributor, and quite often significant passages from otherwise and unknown and little-read authors are found in albums.' (This translation of his words appears in *Early Autograph Albums in the British Museum*. See 'Further Reading'.) The most famous of the early collectors was Ludwig van Beethoven and his book is still in existence.

Very old autograph album

By the late 1700s in Europe it was popular to collect letters of famous people, particularly those in the fields of politics and religion, and the custom of collecting signed works probably spread to Britain and also to America through immigrants. The autograph books as we know them today seem to have their roots in the mid to late 1880s, dating from the 'celebrity cult' which came storming in during the late Victorian era. This was the time when music hall artistes such as Marie Lloyd and Vesta Tilley became famous and enthusiasts gathered at stage doors in the hope that a star would sign their book or give them an autographed photograph. Presumably this was when special small books especially intended for the collection of autographs became more commonplace and people realised that this was a good hobby, even if they didn't know anyone famous. They could get their friends to write affectionate or uplifting verses, amusing rhymes and thoughtful quotes, to make both attractive collections as well as keepsakes. General Montgomery kept an autograph album which contained a page of notes by Sir Winston Churchill as well as the signatures of many important people from the war years. Later, his autograph book was deemed so interesting that it was published as a memento of the Second World War.

Collecting the autographs of friends became a very popular pastime, continuing right up until the 1980s, before dwindling when texting, computers and other electronic gadgets took over from the written word. These 'autographs' very often involved sentimental, humorous, sad, clever or silly rhymes, while many old albums contain exquisite paintings or drawings. Sometimes they also have photographs, or even small objects such as postage stamps, silks, cigarette cards, buttons, and locks of hair or matchsticks pasted in with witty comments penned beneath. With the advent of the cinema, radio and television, autographs from popular stars were keenly sought, and people started to build up collections of autograph books filled solely with the names or the photos of famous people. In the case of highly popular stars, especially some of the film stars and top musicians, the demand for signatures grew so much that

photos would often be signed by secretaries or family members, rather than the celebrities themselves.

Sadly, although there are some celebrities who still enjoy signing autographs freely for their fans, a growing number have become wary, mainly due to traders who will ask for several autographs at once and then sell them. That is why many stars will only sign at charity events where collectors must pay for a signature, or will only sign the autograph books of young children. It must be infuriating, almost degrading, for a celebrity to sign an autograph for someone they know has absolutely no interest in him, his films or his music, but just sees him as a way to earn money. Even worse, some dealers discover a celebrity's home address and write to him, bombarding him with requests, or even stand outside his home armed with photos for signing. It often must be difficult for a celebrity to know whether the person requesting the signature is really a trader, or just a fan who genuinely wants several autographs for his friends. American boxer George Foreman actually keeps a record of every person who has written for an autograph, reasoning that if they do it several times they must be a trader. Even so, many traders are honest, and the stars get to know them and realising they have to make a living too, will good-naturedly sign several photos. It just depends on the star in question.

Children tend to enjoy collecting autographs of people, even those who are just a little bit famous; players in local football teams, amateur actors or local councillors, for example, and they often stand a better chance of obtaining a star's autograph, than does an adult. Frequently a celebrity will make time for a child, even if he is in a hurry and even those who rarely sign can make an exception for a child. Sometimes children get the chance to obtain celebrity autographs through their schools when authors come and give talks or children's entertainers come to open fetes or present prizes.

The autographs of top personalities, especially those who have chosen to rarely sign, can fetch large sums, while the death of a celebrity can result in a temporary rise in autograph prices – though they normally return to a sensible price later. It depends on the star, and whether he is a 'legend'. Some signatures not only of stars but also of royalty or people of historical importance, can sell for thousands of pounds.

Where do people find autographs?

As already mentioned, autographs of the famous can be obtained from many sources. They can be collected in person from stage doors, book signings or public appearances, by writing to a celebrity, or bought from various dealers. The easiest way to build up a collection of the signatures of us lesser mortals, though, is to ask around family, friends and neighbours for old, unwanted autograph albums. A good source is in attics and lofts (with permission, of course), as they frequently house old books and papers. I have acquired family autograph albums and autographed Bibles by letting it be known amongst my relatives that I was building a collection. Another way of obtaining the books is from boot sales, collectors' fairs, antiques centres or from the internet. If it is the rhymes which interest you, then you shouldn't have to pay more than a few pounds for an old (Edwardian or earlier) album. It is only when the albums contain many fine paintings, have military or other specialised interests, or contain signatures of famous people that prices escalate.

To me the fascination of autograph albums is to read all those entries from a bygone era; so sweet and innocent, so touching and heart warming. They were written in more leisurely days before computers and mobile phones when people had time to think and to compose an eloquent verse or piece of prose, or to inscribe one of the numerous rhymes which, judging by the number of times they crop up, everyone seemed to know at the time. Verses such as 'Your Album is a Garden which only Friends May Know', 'Make New Friends but Keep the Old', 'When You Get Married and Have Twins', 'By Hook or by Crook' and the ubiquitous 'Roses are Red' with its numerous variations are seen time and again.

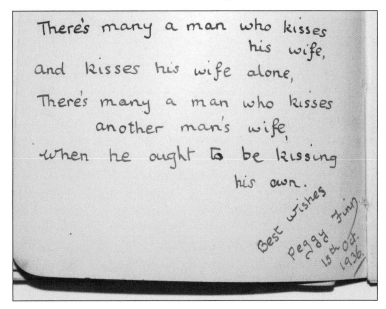

Meeting 'Grotbags' (Carol Lee Scott) at a school fete

Forget-me-not flowers crop up in albums the most, though roses and violets are also exceedingly popular. Love, marriage and babies are recurrent themes, which is unsurprising considering the majority of autograph books were owned by young women or schoolgirls. Friendship is another popular topic with people proclaiming undying devotion. It's interesting to analyse the themes. Broadly speaking they fall into four distinct categories. Firstly, there are the flippant, humorous or novelty entries – the verses and drawings which usually bear no relevance to the owner of the album but are purely entries chosen to entertain. Secondly, there are the sentimental entries – these often proclaim friendship, love or advice. The third type consists of quotes, homilies, texts or poems. Sometimes these poems seem original to the writer, but more often are an extract from a well-known poet such as Browning, Shakespeare, Kipling, or Keats. The fourth category belongs to those entries that I think of as 'self indulgent'. These are the self-satisfied, holier-than-thou entries that were particularly in vogue in Edwardian times and up to the 1920s. You can imagine these being written by elderly aunts with pursed mouths like cats' bottoms, or pompous uncles who believed that their flighty nieces needed a firm hand to keep them on the straight and narrow. They tended to write moralistic verses and prose which set out their rules for behaviour, and you can imagine the young recipient screwing up her nose in disgust as she read the offering.

Looking through the entries from albums collected here, it's difficult to choose favourites, but I think my vote for simplicity and delightful sentiment must go to the popular, 'If friends were flowers, then I would pick you.' If a friend wrote that in my album, then I would feel honoured. My own albums tended to contain the more prosaic verses such as 'By hook or by crook, I'll be first in this book.' In fairness, though, I probably wasn't any more imaginative when I wrote in my friends' books. I was ten when I was filling up my own autograph books as a child and collected into my early teens. However, in earlier decades, I think that many of the autograph albums were owned by young women in their late teens because at that time and age they were more erudite and thoughtful than us 1950s' school kids. Comparison of a 1920s' book to one from the 1950s reveals an enormous difference. The 1920s' book contains numerous entries - many of them very long - as well as sketches, paintings and even novelty items such as silk threads or postage stamps. The writing is usually exquisite. In contrast, the entries in 1950s' book are mainly banal with untidy writing, often a lazy scrawl.

Why do people collect autographs?

When you think about it, it seems rather odd to want to obtain and cherish a scrap of paper on which someone has scribbled their name. What's the point? What makes that piece of paper special? I suppose the main attraction, certainly with regard to anyone famous or in the public eye, is that with that scrap of paper you are holding something on which the celebrity has had to focus his mind for a few seconds. You have shared his world. He spared time from his busy schedule to personally do something just for you. He wrote his name and by doing so and giving it to you, you have the proof. You also have proof, of course, that you met him or communicated with him in some way, or have bought a snippet of his life. By owning an autograph it feels as though you have secured a fragment of the star's time and it gives you a warm glow, especially when that star is someone you particularly admire.

The reasons for collecting old autograph albums are slightly different, as are the reasons for starting up an autograph album of your own for the collection of signatures of friends and relatives. The latter is a sentimental keepsake for within the album are names of people you love, or loved, who have taken the trouble to write an amusing or uplifting verse for you. Looking back on one of these books after several years can be a moving experience, because by then many of those people of whom you were so fond might have passed away, or have lost touch. If you remember to ask new friends to add their names, your book eventually becomes a documentary of your life. However, those of us who collect old autograph albums belonging to people they have never known are something of an enigma. Why do we do it? Is there any point of collecting books of rhymes written by strangers, probably long gone, with names we will never trace?

I suppose that the reason we do it – certainly in my case – is for the intriguing light it throws upon the social history of past decades, for instance an old autograph book dating from before the First World War. Usually these books are quite small, around six inches by five inches. Run your finger over the cover. It will probably be covered in a dark-coloured cloth or leather – green, blue, black or magenta – and it will have the word 'Autographs' written in gold lettering across the front. Sometimes there might be a small picture on the cover, too. Where did the book originally come from? Was it a Christmas or birthday gift? We probably won't ever know, though sometimes there is a clue inside. An inscription perhaps, from the donor, together with a date, or maybe the new owner will have written her name and date on the inside cover. If it's a December or early-January date, it's odds on it was a Christmas gift. Just think of all the people who have touched that cover over the years. No wonder it's looking rather worse for wear.

Everyone who signed their name will have handled that book and the owner will have spent many hours thumbing through the pages, reliving her memories. No doubt she treasured the book all her life until she died. Hopefully, the book would have passed on down through the family, but more often it will find its way to a dealer, charity shop or flea market, waiting for a sympathetic collector to come along and give it a new home. Inside the pages will probably be coloured in pastel shades of blue, green, pink, beige or lemon, presumably because it was felt less intimidating and more encouraging to write on a coloured sheet than a stark, white one. If you are lucky, the book will be filled with a variety of rhymes, quotes, sayings, and amusing comments, all signed and dated. If you are very fortunate, there will also be sketches and watercolours too. The creativity of people a few decades ago was truly extraordinary.

Autograph collecting can be enjoyed by anybody, old or young, rich or poor, from all walks of life and of any nationality. It can be a cheap hobby unless you are a collector of rare letters or signed memorabilia. All you need is an autograph book and a pen. It can be a great way to record a

BLOW!

Will. F. Ordish, Derby.
1909

special event, maybe a wedding or a family reunion. By recording the signatures from the guests you will have a unique record of the occasion, something which will become part of your family history. If you are a really keen autograph hunter, you could have a series of themed books, keeping categories separate for actors, musicians, sportsmen and politicians.

Nowadays because we all use computers, printers and telephones, the hand-written document is becoming much rarer and we tend to sign our names much less than we once did. Looking back at the old autograph books, most of the entries were made using an impeccable hand, were often ornate, and were written with a fountain pen or dip pen. Today ballpoint or felt tip pen is used to scrawl our names, and on the rare occasions we need to hand-write a letter, we find we need to concentrate really hard to ensure we make it neat and legible. So perhaps it's more important than ever that we begin collecting autographs, thus giving our friends and relatives much needed writing practice!

When you are asked to sign an autograph book, there is much to think about. It's certainly not a task to be undertaken lightly. Firstly, you must select your page. If you rhyme is one which has to be inscribed on the first

or last pages, then, providing they haven't already been taken, it's easy to choose. However, if your rhyme or homily can be inscribed on any page, then you have the problem of deciding which page you will honour with your signature. Many autograph books are made up of pastel-coloured pages, so you need to choose your favourite colour, decide whereabouts in the book you would like to be (I always find the middle very comforting!) and decide whether you want a right hand side or left hand side page. Will you write in pencil, ink, ballpoint or felt tip? Have you devised a special signature for use on these occasions? Maybe one with swirls or extra large ornamental capital letters? And when you have determined all that, then comes the decision of what to write! Hopefully, you will gain inspiration from the entries and ideas in the following chapters.

A Philographist's Prayer
Can't think,
Brain numb,
Inspiration won't come,
Can't write,
Bad pen,
Much love,
Amen

CHAPTER TWO

Amusing quotations and entertaining rhymes, found in autograph books of the late nineteenth century to the 1940s

THERE WAS PLENTY of humour around, especially in books dating from the First World War. There was also much patriotism at this time. Many of the earlier rhymes were sentimental or very solemn, and most of these can be found in Chapter 3 – the majority of the entries here are light hearted. (The date following each rhyme is when the entry which I found was made in the autograph book; the actual rhyme or quote might be years, decades or even centuries earlier. Where known, the original author of the quote is shown in brackets after the quote).

Animals, Gardens, Seasons, Weather

In the storms of life
When you need an umbrella
May you have it held it up
By a handsome young fella.
1933

> *The umbrella is an ancient invention, and is depicted in sculpture on ancient monuments. They were popular in France from the mid 1700s, though the English didn't take to them till the 1800s. The word umbrella is derived from the Latin word umbra meaning shade.*

It is a sign that winter has gone
When the birds begin to sing

But when a girl sits on a pin
It's a sign of an early spring.
1908

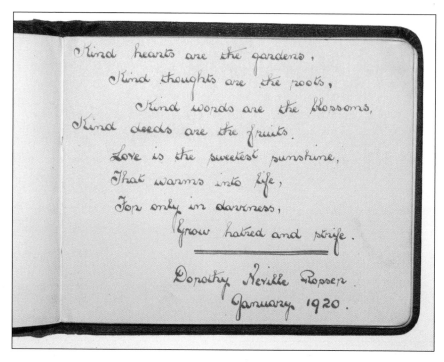

Kind hearts are the garden.
Kind thoughts are the roots.
Kind words are the blossoms.
Kind deeds are the fruits.
1900s

Look at the plants in the garden
Speak of the birds that sing
But when you sit on a red hot poker
It's the sign of an early spring.
1920s

Oh primrose time is pleasant
But September is the best,
When the purple berries cluster
Around the robin's nest,
And nuts are on the hazel
And acorns on the oak,
And the shady woods are tempting
To the shyest fairy folk,
Out then, quick then,
Berry pickers all,

Though bramble thorns may prick you
And the rain showers fall.
1900s

Paddling down the stream of life
In your very own canoe
May you have such pleasant times
And plenty of room for two
1924

> *Canoes were developed by the Native Americans, and the word originated from 'kenu' which means dugout. The first canoes were made from large shaped and hollowed tree trunks, strong enough to travel between the islands.*

Shine like a glow worm if you can't be a star
1920s

Sing you a song in the garden of life
If you only gather a thistle
Sing you a song as you travel along
If you can't sing, just whistle
1926

The fox loves the valley
And the deer loves the hill
The boys love the girls
And I'm sure they always will.
1940s

WISH I HAD A CORKSCREW!

The rain it raineth on the just
And also on the unjust fella
But mainly on the just because
The unjust steals the just's umbrella
1930s

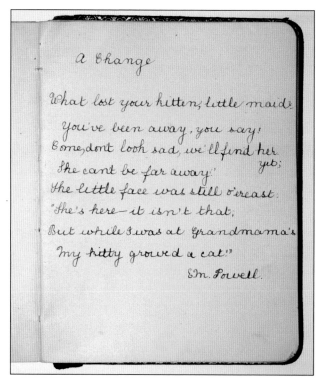

What lost your kitten, little maid?
You've been away, you say.
Come, don't look sad, we'll find her yet,
She can't be far away.
The little face was still o'ercast,
"She's here. It isn't that.
But while I was at Grandmama's
My kitty growed a cat"!
1900s

Courtship and Marriage

A tablespoon's a clumsy thing
A teaspoon is far nicer
But of all the spoons upon this earth
The sofa spoons the sweetest
1920s

'And am I the first girl you ever
made love to?' asked the lady's
maid of her valet lover.
'Well', was the reply, 'I've pressed suits before, you know.'
1914

As sure as comes your wedding day,
A broom to you I'll send,
In sunshine use the bushy part,
In storm the other end.
1896

Queen Victoria began the present day fashion of wearing white as the wedding dress, though for years afterwards, a poorer bride still made do with wearing her best dress, whatever the colour.

Definition of Love
A tickling of the heart that cannot be scratched
1906

Don't try kissing
When you're swinging on a gate
1920s

Fall from a housetop
Fall from above
Fall from anywhere
But don't fall in love
1912

Fall from the top of some high tree
Fall from a cliff above
Fall from a 'bike' and break your neck
But never fall in love
Don't do as I do but do as I tell you
1904

He criticised her pudding
He didn't like her cake
He wished she'd make the biscuits
That his mother used to make
She didn't wash the dishes
She didn't make the stew
And she didn't darn his linen
As his mother used to do
Oh well she wasn't perfect
Though she always tried her best
Then one day at length she thought
It was time to have a rest
So when that day he scolded
The same complaints all through
She turned around and boxed his ears
Like his mother used to do
1920

How it Happened:
He and She
Had some Tea
Then a Walk
And a Talk
Again Met
Nothing Yet
Maiden Joy
Bashful Boy
Weather Wet
Don't Fret
She said Come
To my Home
A nice Settee
Just you and Me
So they Sat

A loving Pat
From the Girl
Head in Whirl
Lights all Out
His heart Stout
He to she, marry Me
She to he, got the Fee?
He said Yes
Squeeze a Kiss.
One Year Gone
There Upon
Same Settee
Now are Three
1920s

I wish I was a china cup
From which you take your tea
For every time you take a sup
'T would mean a kiss for me
1926

If John marries Mary and Mary alone
Tis a very good match between Mary and John
Should John wed a score, oh the claws and the scratches
It can't be a match: 'tis a bundle of matches!
(Cowper)
1906

In 1827, a chemist called John Walker found that by coating the end of a stick with various chemicals and leaving them to dry, striking the stick caused a flame. He called them 'Congreves', and later they became marketed as 'Lucifers'. In 1855, a Swede, Johan Edvard Lundström, produced the first red phosphorus 'safety' matches.

In a parlour there were three
A maid, a parlour lamp and he
Two's company without a doubt
And so the parlour lamp went out
1936

Men are April when they woo
December when they wed
Maids are May when they are maids
But the sky changes when they are wives.
(Shakespeare)
1919

Never make love in a cornfield.
Remember corn has ears.
1936

Never make love in an onion patch
It will always end in tears.
1950s

Never make love in a narrow lane
It will always end in a tight
squeeze.
1936

Never make love in a potato patch
Remember potatoes have eyes.
1930s

For centuries people credited Sir Walter Raleigh with introducing potatoes to England, but now historians suspect that Sir Francis Drake brought them back from the Aztecs.

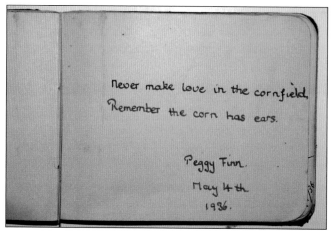

Never make love in the cornfield,
Remember the corn has ears.

Peggy Finn.
May 4th.
1936.

Only One Look
Hand in Hand
Heart to Heart
Just a few more Kisses
Before we Part
But soon there comes
A Happy Day
When no more Good-Byes we'll say
1920s

Pick up the glove, drop the 'g',
What is left I give to thee.
1924

Olive C Stringer
31-1-1912

" Mummy, may I get married?"
" Why, dear?"
" Oh, just to amuse the children;
they've never seen a wedding".

Recipe for Love Cake
First take one small seat. 1 long arm, 1 head on shoulder, 2 little hesitations. Stir slowly. Then add 1 May 2 six kisses.
1920s
(Presumably, the last sentence should be read as 'one May to six kisses' – the lucky receiver of six kisses was a lady named May.)

Some girls love their brothers
But I so good have grown
That I love somebody else's
Better than my own.
1920s

There's many a man who kisses his wife
And kisses his wife alone
There's many a man who kisses another man's wife
When he ought to be kissing his own.
1936

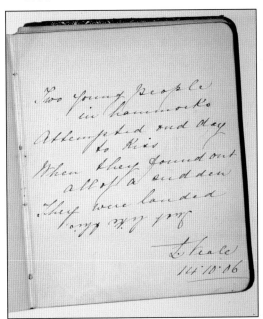

Two young people in
   hammocks
Attempted one day to
   kiss
When they found out, all
   of a sudden
They were landed
sıɥʇ ǝʞıl ʇsnɾ
1906

Hammocks probably originated approximately 1,000 years ago in Central America. Columbus brought them to Europe after discovering their uses by natives of the Bahamas. Soon, canvas hammocks began to be used by sailors – but the Navy ones were just 4 inches wide.

Two on a stile attempted to kiss
In less than a moment they were
ʇsnſ ǝʞᴉl ʇɥᴉs
1920s

Cynicism and Self-deprecation

A pretty miss
A crowded car
Pray take my seat
And there you are

A crowded car
A woman plain
She stands
And there you are again
1906

Looping the Loop.

Presumably the car referred to here was a tramcar. The Blackpool electric tram service opened in September 1885. Soon trams were commonplace in many British towns, though most have long since disappeared. However, the Blackpool trams still run today.

At three years of age we love our mothers
At six our fathers, at ten holidays
At sixteen, dress, at twenty our sweethearts
At twenty-five our wives
At forty our children
At sixty – ourselves
1907

Awfully sorry I've nothing to write
about, so can only add my
signature which is pretty rotten,
too.
1931

Cash governs the world and the
world governs the man
The man governs the woman but
the woman rules the man
She also rocks the infant and
teaches it how to trot

So when you come to reckon it up
It's woman that governs the lot
1910

Comforting!:
Visitor (in the sickroom)
'I just looked in to cheer you up a bit, and I'm very glad I did, because
I met the doctor going out and he says you're much worse than you
think you are, and unless you keep your spirits up you can't recover.'
1911

(Name) is a peach, they say.
Well, she is one, I'll own.
Her face is like its glowing blush
Her heart within – a stone.
1930s

The women tell me every day
That all my bloom has past away
'Behold', the pretty wantons cry,
'Behold this mirror with a sigh;
The locks upon thy brow are few,
And, like the rest, they're withering too!'

Whether age-time has thinn'd my hair,
I'm sure I neither know nor care;
But this I know, and this I feel,
As onward to the tomb I steal,
That still as death approaches nearer,
The joys of life are sweeter, dearer;
And had I but an hour to live,
That bitter hour to bless I'd give.
(Anacreon)
1918

The Odes of Anacreon, were written by Anacreon, a Greek poet who lived between 570 and 488 BC. He was especially notable for his drinking songs and hymns. An anecdote by Pliny the Elder has it that he choked on a grape stone and died, but this could well be apocryphal. Centuries later, the odes were translated. The version here was by Thomas Moore.

I am not troubled by my neighbour's chickens now, since every night I put a lot of eggs in the grass very carefully, & every morning when he was looking I went out & brought them in.

Amy Stringa

This world is not so bad
  a place
As some would try to
  make it;
Though whether good
  or whether bad
Depends on how we
  take it.
1909

"Now I'll win her"

There is much for which to be
  thankful
In this jolly old world of ours -
After the storm comes sunshine
And after the winter comes flowers
If I find a hole in my stocking,
I'm thankful it's not in my shoe!
I'm thankful there's only one war on –

Imagine if there were two!
But oh! I should cease to be
  thankful
If ever it came to pass
That I looked as I sometimes
  appear in
A taxi cab looking-glass.
1918

Trust ye in no man
Not even thy brother
Girls, if you must love
Love one another!
1933

When you have chosen the proper way
And the proper thing to do
There is always someone ready to say
I wouldn't if I were you.
1911

Food

A Grace for an Ice Cream:
For ice-cream cheap but good,
That finds us in a thirsty mood;
For ices made of milk and cream
That slides down smoothly as a
  dream;
For cornets, sandwiches and pies
That make the gastric juices rise;

For ices bought in little shops
Or at the kerb from him who stops;
For chanting of the sweet refrain:
'Vanilla, strawberry or plain?'
We thank thee Lord, who sends
  with heat
This cool deliciousness to eat.
1930s

The type of ice cream we're familiar with today was created in the eighteenth century, and its ingredients are cream, egg yolks, sugar and milk. Before then it would have been a form of sorbet or water ice. During the 1920s, right up to the 1950s, the Walls' company used bicycles to sell their produce, bearing the slogan 'Stop Me and Buy One', while, slightly earlier, the 'Hokey-Pokey' man with his ice cream was a welcome sight for children.

Beef when you are hungry
Bass when you are dry
A nice boy to sleep with
And Heaven when you die.
1930s

Give us a shout!
Give us a cheer!
Give us a pub!
And give us the beer!
1940s

Look not thou upon the wine when it is red,
When it giveth its colour in the cup,
At the last it biteth like a serpent
And stingeth like an adder.
(Prov. 23:31-5)
1920s

The cats take to gardening.

Love is like a mutton chop
Sometimes cold.
Sometimes hot
Whether cold or whether hot
It's not a thing to be forgot.
1920s

No glory I covet
No riches I want
Ambition is nothing to me
But one thing I ask
Kind heaven to grant
After dinner a good cup of tea.
1920s

Love is like a mutton chop
Sometimes cold and sometimes hot
Love is heavenly
Love is strong
So is mutton when kept too long.
1930s

Patent Desired:
O that some bright adventurous man
Would patent, make and sell
An onion with an onion taste
But with a violet smell.
1907

The End of the Onions:
We are all cut up in slices,
Thick and thin, in queer devices
And we're nothing like the chaps we used to be,
We are so mixed up together
That it is quite uncertain whether
I, the teller of the tale, am really me.

We have lost our clothes for ever,
And I fear that we shall never,
Nevermore grow manly whiskers on our chins
Yet the girl who spoilt our beauty
Did it only as a duty,
And I saw that she was sorry for her sins.
For her eyes grew very tearful
When she saw that we were fearful
And her face was full of pity for our pain,
And if anything can cheer us,
And make things warmer for us
It's the thought of sympathetic Mary Jane.
1900s

> *Onions were worshipped by the ancient Egyptians who believed that its spherical shape and concentric rings symbolised eternal life, and that the strong scent would bring life back to the dead. Roman gladiators rubbed onion on their skins to firm up their muscles, while athletes in ancient Greece believed onion would 'lighten the balance of the blood'.*

When I was young and in my prime
I could eat a teacake in no time
But now I'm old and turning grey
It nearly takes me half a day
1929

Men and women

Fair woman was made to bewitch
A blessing, a curse, a companion, a nurse
Fair woman was made to be which.
1918

He. "Of course, ladies are much more handsome than men."
She. "Naturally."
He. "No, artificially."
1909

Her eyes she got from her father
Her nose from her mother meek
But where in all creation
Did she get her blessed cheek?
1900s

Make the doors upon a woman's wit, and it will out at the casement.
Shut that, and 'twill out at the keyhole. Stop that 'twill fly with the
smoke out at the chimney.
(Shakespeare)
1906

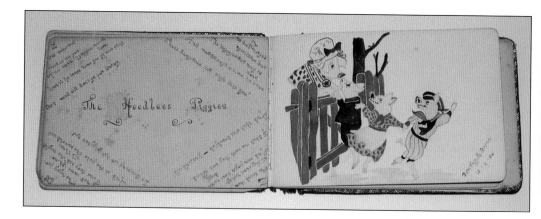

THE NURSERY TRAIN.

From nursery corner starts this baby train,
When they can't go out because of the rain

Dick and Dot and Sue and Jane,
Round the nursery and back again.

Man wants but little here below and is not hard to please
But Woman bless her little heart wants Everything she sees.
And half of what she don't see.
1920s

The lady who sent this rhyme says 'I've a feeling that the writer might have added the last line himself...I'm pretty sure he was a he...I don't think a woman would write that somehow!'

Men have many faults
Women have but two
There's nothing good in what they say
And nothing right they do
1930s
(Unfortunately, this entry was just initialled so it's impossible to tell if written by a man or women – it's not particularly flattering to either sex.)

Patience is a virtue
Possess it if you can
Often found in a woman
But seldom in a man.
1920s

Quite a Sight:
I am sorry to say
Miss Annabel Grey
Oft spoke to her friends
In a very rude way

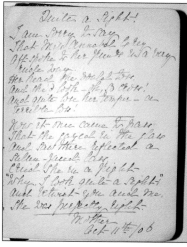

Her head she would toss
And she would look, oh, so cross!
And quite lose her temper,
A terrible loss!

Now it once came to pass
That she gazed in the glass
And saw there reflected a sullen-
faced lass
Cried she in a fright
"Why, I look quite a sight"
And betwixt you and me
She was perfectly right!
1906

Time they say will wait for no man
And the moments pass away
Weeks and months still follow quickly
As the time goes by each day
1912

When God made the world
He made the man the strongest
But to give the woman a chance
He made her tongue the longest.
1920

When God made the world
He made the man first
Then he made woman
And rectified all his mistakes.
1923

When lads have money
They think they're men
But when they've none
They're lads again
1943

Patriotic and Political

By Jingo, I'll be the first as you
can see.
1914

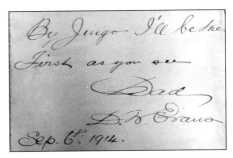

This variation to 'By Hook and By Crook' (See Chapter 4) was written by my great grandfather in his daughter's book. According the 'Shorter Oxford Dictionary', the phrase 'By Jingo' was derived from a conjuror's chant, and later appeared in a popular patriotic song in the late 1800s.

England was Hungary
Had a piece of Turkey
On a bit of China
Dipped in Greece
1920s

How to Cook A German Sausage:
Cook on a British Kitchener
Greece well with Russian tallow
Flavour with a little Jellicoe
Servia up with French capons and Brussels scouts
1914

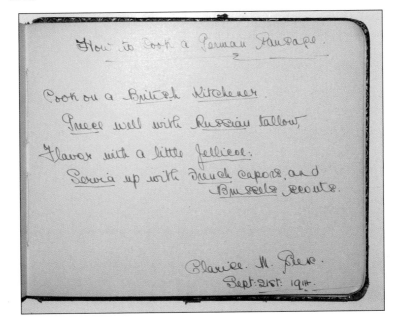

The world is a bundle of hay
Mankind are the asses who pull;
Each tugs in a different way
And the greatest of all is
John Bull
(Byron)
1920s

Recipe for Cabinet Pudding:
Take a fresh young Suffragist, add a large idea of her own importance
and as much sauce as you like. Allow her to stand on a Cabinet
Minister's doorstep until in a white heat. Mix with one or two
policeman, well roll in the mud and when hot run into a Police Court
and allow to simmer. Garnish with sauce of martyrdom. Popular dish
– always in season. Lost – a little self respect.
1908

*Suffragettes wanted the right for women to vote, and the movement
was started by Millicent Fawcett in 1897. Six years later, Emmeline
Pankhurst and her daughters Christabel and Sylvia founded the
Women's Social and Political Union. Thousands of women joined,
sometimes using violence to try to achieve their aim.*

"more haste less speed."

Olive Morley
December 21st 1907

Quirkiness

The Dug-Out Motto:
He who ducks and runs away,
Lives to fight another day,
But he who's reckless and shows his head,
Latest 'bullet-in': he's dead.
1916

He who fights and runs away
Will live to fight another day
He who fights and stands his ground
Will get his blinking clock knocked round.
1920s

Remember me in all your wishes,
Remember me when doing dishes,
And if the water is too hot,
Put in a sweet forget-me-not.
1896

Though shalt not covert thy neighbour's wife
His ox thou shalt not slaughter
But thank the Lord it isn't a sin
To covet they neighbour's daughter.
1910

Two little boys late one night
Tried to get to school on the end of a kite.
The kite string broke
And down they fell.
And instead of school
They went to . . .
Now don't get exited
And don't go pale.
Instead of school,
They went to jail
1930s
(Obviously the missing word was 'hell', still a word not used in polite
society as a cuss word in those days.)

> *Kites have been known for a many centuries. Some people assert that leaf kites were known thousands of years ago in Indonesia. It is known that silk and bamboo kites were use in China almost three thousand years ago, and later, paper kites were used too.*

Travel

Better late than never
Tis a comforting refrain
Save when you reach the station
Just in time to lose the train.
1920s

I dreamt one night to hell I did go
Where did you come from they wanted to know
I've just come from (local town) Station I did grin
You're the first one from there so you had better come in.
1920s

I dreamt I was dead and to Heaven did go
Where I had come from they wanted to know
I said I'm from (name of town)

44

St Peter did stare
He said Jump in quick you're the first one from there
1920

I will not doubt, though all my ships at sea
Come drifting home with broken masts and sails!
I will believe the hand that never fails,
From seeming evil worketh good for me!
And though I weep because those sails are tattered
Still will I say, While my best hope lie shattered
'I trust in Thee'
1920s

Jack and Jill
In a train fulfil
The lighting regulations
But neither mind
That lowered blind
Make them pass their stations
1923

Love many.
Trust few.
Learn to paddle
Your own canoe.
1912

She rocked the boat
And wouldn't you bet
(Name) couldn't float
And she got all wet
In the river's flow
And then (name) shrank

o

o

o

o

The bubbles show
Just where (name) sank
1922

There's many a ship been lost at sea
For want of a keel and a rudder
There's many a girl who has lost her love
Through spooning with another
1930s

Useful rhymes

It's not the man that knows the most
That has the most to say
Nor yet the man that has the most
That gives the most away.
1908

May she to whom this book belongs
Light trials meet (if any).
Her hours of gloom, may they be few
Her sunny moments many.
1919

My heart is like a cabbage
Divided into two.
The leaves I give to anyone,
My heart I give to you.
1907

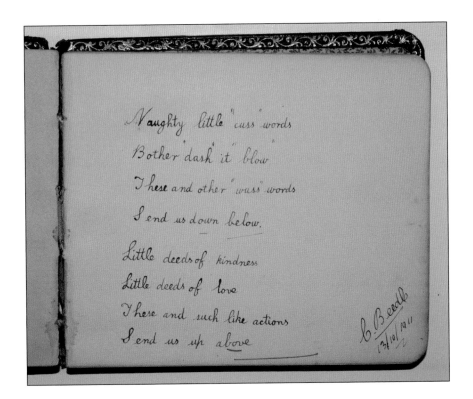

> *Cabbages are not only an excellent source of vitamin C, but also used in European folk medicine to treat acute inflammation, often in a paste but sometimes laying the leaves directly onto the skin.*

Naughty little cuss words
Bother, dash and blow
These and other wuss words
Send us down below

Little deeds of kindness
Little deeds of love
These and suchlike actions
Send us up above
1911

Some people come into our lives and quickly go.
Some stay for a while and leave footprints on our hearts.
1930s

Touch not this book for
Fear of shame
For in it is the owner's name
If you do the Lord will say
'Where is the book you stole away?'
And if you say you do not know
The Lord will say, 'Go down below'.
1919

We live but in the present.
The future is unknown:
Tomorrow is a mystery
Today is all our own.
1940s

CHAPTER THREE

Thoughtful quotations, beautiful verses and enchanting rhymes found in autograph books of the late nineteenth century, up until the 1950s

THESE ARE THE album entries which have obviously been given much thought by their writers. In several cases one wonders why they had been entered in what was meant to be a friendly book owned by someone they presumably were fond of. However, a few flippant rhymes have found their way in here too. As before, the dates relate to the entry I found in the book but the sentiments could be much older.

Admittance and Declaration

Grumble? No! What's the good?
If it availed, I would:
But it doesn't a bit
Not it

Laugh? Yes! Why not?
T'is better that crying a lot;
We were made to be glad
Not sad.

Sing? Why yes, to be sure!
We shall better endure

If the heart's full of song
All the day long.
1925

I love everything that's Old
Old friends, Old times,
Old manners, Old books,
Old wine
1926

I would be true, for there are those who trust me,
I would be pure, for there are those who care,
I would be strong, for there is much to suffer,
I would be brave, for there is much to dare,
I would be friends to all the foe, the friendless,
I would be giving and forget the gift,
I would be humble, for I know my weakness,
I would look up, and laugh and love – and lift
(Howard Arnold Walter)
1920s

Parting is such sweet sorrow;
I could say goodbye until tomorrow,
Yet, to part would be too much pain
To think we never would meet again.
1900s

Advice

A cheery word – a cheery smile
The fast they foot it for many a mile
With what bright glamour
And what sweet guile
They make home Heaven
And life worthwhile.
1919

I should make an excellent Turk
For I was never gifted for work
But devoted to tobacco and ladies.
1904

The smile is formed by flexing the muscles near both ends of the mouth. When the eye muscles are also involved, it is known as a Duchenne smile. Although in humans it denotes happiness or pleasure, in animals a similar expression can be a threat, warning, sign of submission or of fear.

Always eat when you are hungry
Always drink when you are dry
Always sleep when you are tired
But don't stop breathing or you'll die!
1920

Be a good girl
Lead a good life
Get a good husband
Make a good wife
1928

Be good, sweet maid, and let who will be clever;
Do noble things, not dream them, all day long
And so make life, death and that for ever
One grand sweet song.
(Charles Kingsley)
1912
(*See also 'Eat well, sweet maid', Chapter 5*)

Before you speak of other's faults
Pray think about your own
They who in glass houses live
Should never throw a stone
1929

Curved is the line of beauty
Straight is the line of duty
Walk by the last and then shalt see
The other ever follow thee.
1900s

Defer not to tomorrow to be wise
Tomorrow's sun to thee may never rise
1920s

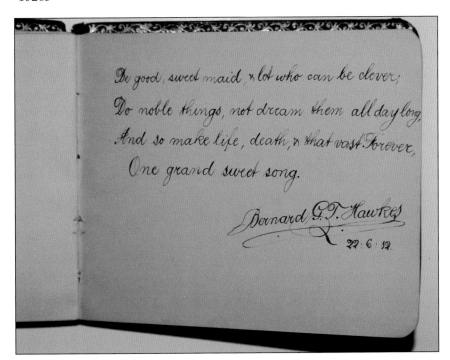

Don't look for the flaws as you go through life
And even when you find them
It is well and kind to be somewhat blind
And to look for the virtue behind them.
The world will never adjust itself
To suit your whines to the letter
Some things must go wrong your whole life long
And the sooner you know it the better
1919

Do not save your kindness
For to-morrow's sky,
For the souls who need you
Now are passing by;
Live your best this moment,
That's the better way;
Serve the Christ with purpose,
Just today, today.
1909

Go placidly amid the noise and haste
And remember what peace there may be in silence.
(Max Ehrmann)
1989

God has not promised
Life without pain
Light without shadow
Sun without rain

But he has promised
Strength from above
Unfailing sympathy
Undying LOVE
(*Written in my daughter's
album by her grandmother*)
1989

He that waits to do a great deal at once will never do anything
1931

If a string is in a knot,
Patience can untie it.
Patience can do many things.
Did you ever try it?
1900s

A form of string was used in Palaeolithic times for tying, bags,
clothing, bowstrings and for fishing nets.

If thy heart offend thee, chastise it with thy mind
1904

If you can't be a pine on the top of a hill
Be a scrub in the valley but be
The best little scrub on the side of the hill
Be a bush if you can't be a tree
If you can't be a tree be a bit of the grass
And come highway happiness make
If you can't be a muskie then just be a bass
But the liveliest bass in the lake!
1935

A muskie or muskellunge is a large North American fish, also found
in lakes in Canada. Muskies are the largest members of the pike family,
and have elongated bodies, flat heads and fins set well back. They are
light silver, green or brown and have dark stripes or spots on their flanks,
and can grow to almost 5 ft.

If you've a mother with silver hair
If you've a mother treat her with care
And when you grow older the least you can do
Is the same for your mother as she did for you.
1936

If you your lips would keep from slips
Five things observe with care
To whom you speak
Of whom you speak
And how and when and where
1936

If wisdom's ways you wisely seek
Observe five things with care
To whom you speak
Of whom you speak
Why, when and where
1928

It's a very good world to live in
To lend, to spend, to give in
But to borrow, or beg, or to claim
  one's own
It's the very worst world
That ever was known
1924

It's easy enough to be pleasant
When life flows along with a song
But the girl that's worthwhile
Is the one who will smile
When everything goes dead wrong.
1920

Keep your face with sunshine lit
Laugh a little bit
Gloomy shadows oft will flit
If you have the wit and grit
Just to laugh a little bit.
1934

Kindness is love doing little
things, things that seem scarcely
worth doing and yet which
mean much to those for whom they are wrought.
1904

Never quit the natural; it forms a complete style.
1916

Patience et longueur de temps
Font plus qui force ni que rage
(Patience and length of time do more than force or rage.)
1919

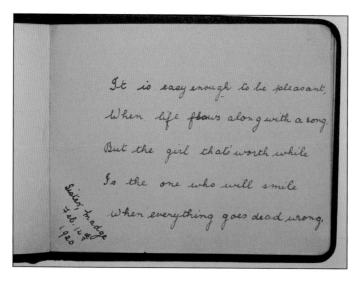

Smile at the world in passing
Sunshiny weather or rain
For a smile leaves an increase behind it
And you will not be passing again
1912

'T ain't what we have,
But what we give,
'T ain't what we are,
But how we live,
'T ain't what we do,
But how we do it,
That makes life worth
Going through it.
1931

Ten Rules of Life:
Never put off tomorrow what you can do today
Never trouble others for what you can do yourself
Never spend your money before you have it
Never buy what you do not want because it is cheap
Pride costs more than hunger, thirst and cold
We never repent of having eaten too little
Nothing is troublesome that we do willingly
How much pain have those evils cost us which never happened.
Take things always by their smooth handle
When angry, count ten before you speak, if very angry count one
  hundred.
1908

There is so much good in the worst of us
There is so much bad in the best of us
That it ill becomes any one of us
To speak about the rest of us.
1913

Think of today as the only day as the only day
Never give in to sorrow
It's just as well you never can tell
What may occur tomorrow
It might be better it might be worse

We might never be here at all
So cheer up old chappy
And try to be happy
That's my advice to all
Written by an 80-year-old lady in 1960

This above all
To thine own self be true
And it must follow, as night the day
Thou can'st not then be false to any man.
1900s

Those who are wise press onward
Those who are strong ascend
So be not crushed by a great defeat
But begin again my friend
1935

'Tis only noble to be good
Kind hearts are more than Coronets,
And simple faith than Norman blood'
(Alfred Lord Tennyson)
1913

Whatever you are: Be that
Whatever you say: Be true
Be honest. In fact straightforwardly act
Be nobody else but you.
Give every answer pat,
Your character true unfurl
And when it is ripe
You'll then be a type
Of a typical English girl.
1906

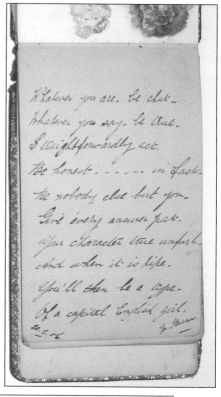

According to Victorian Painter John Collier, 'The typical English girl has something of the boy in her figure. She is not so wide in the hips as the Frenchwoman, the Italian woman, or the Spanish woman, but, on the other hand she is broader on the shoulders…One great beauty of the English girl is the variety of tint her hair assumes. It ranges from dark brown to black, through auburn to red, and from flaxen to almost white.'

Work as though you may live
  forever
Live as though you may die today.
1900s

Your future lies before you
Like a sheet of driven snow
Be careful how you tread it
For every step will show
1922

Epitaphs

Come here and look where I do be
And view the place where I do lie
As you are now so once I be
So prepare yourself to follow me
(Epitaph 1867)
1928

Epitaph in Elgin Cathedral:
Here lie I, Martin Elginbrodde
Hae mercy o' my soul, Lord God,
As I would do, were I Lord God
And ye were Martin Elginbrodde.
1900s

Friends

A friend is a gift you give yourself
1935

A friend is someone who knows the song in your heart and can sing
it back to you when you have forgotten the words.
1953

A friend is someone who knows all your faults but who still likes you.
1939

Choose cautiously thy friends
Observe them well
'Ere thou admit them to thy
  confidence
Then having proved their worth
Hold them fast
For friends are hard to get
But easy lost
1904

Don't walk in front of me.
I may not follow.
Don't walk behind me.
I may not lead
Just walk beside me
And be my friend.
1930s

Friendship:
Forget me not,
Forget me never,
You may change but
I shall never
Though separation be our lot
Dearest (name)
Forget me not.
1908

Friendship is the golden chain
That links our hearts together
And if we never break that chain
We shall be friends forever
1936

Friendship penned these lines
May memory hold them dear
And often bringing to mind
The friend who wrote them here.
1900s

From quiet homes and first beginnings
Out to the undiscovered ends
There's nothing worth the wear of winning
As laughter and the love of friends
(Belloc)
1936

Give me a friend who changes not
Or else no friend at all
Who loves me in my straw thatched cot
As in my marble hall
Who chides me when I do amiss
Who praises where praise is due
Who leads me on in righteousness
And is forever true.
1919

I dip my pen into the ink
And grasp your album tight,
But to save my life
I just can't think
One single word to write
But if writing in an album
Would prove a friend secure
I will with pleasure write
My full name in yours.
1890s

I don't know how she does it
I've never heard her say
But she's got a smile that fits her face
And she wears it every day
You'll know her when you meet her
You'll find it worth your while
To cultivate the friendship
Of the girl behind the smile.
1946

In your golden chain of friends,
    consider me a link.
1927

In your golden chain of memory
Remember me as a link
1909

If friends were flowers, then I
    would pick you.
1952

It's grand to make a name
In history handed down
But I'd rather have part
In a friend's loving heart
Than any great renown
1928

Make new friends, but keep the old,
Those are silver, they are gold,
Brow may wrinkle, hair turn grey,
But true friendship, never know decay.
1900s

Of all the gifts which Heaven bestows
There is one above all measure
And that's a friend midst all the woes
A friend is found a treasure
To thee I give that sacred name
For thou are such to me
And ever proudly will I claim
To be a friend to thee.
1900s

Lest we forget
Ah! No! and yet
Can mem'ry's tie be broken
Our friendship still continue well
Undying, though unspoken.
1930s

May you never meet a friend
In ascending the hill of
     prosperity
1920s

Golden lines so fair and bright.
One by one thy pages fill.
Love and friendship tested gold
Time shall burnish brighter still

Remember me is all I ask
But, if remembrance proves a
    task,
Forget.
1919

Remember M
Remember E
Put them together
And remember ME
1930s

Remember Dave?
Remember Lee?
Well forget them
Remember me!
1950s

Remember me when this you see
And keep me in your mind
Let all the world say what they will
Speak of me as you find.
1922

Round is the ring that has
    no end.
So is my love for you my friend.
(Written in a circle)
1911

Tell me quick
Before I faint
Is we friends
Or is we ain't?
1952

Fainting can be related to fear, severe pain, emotional distress or a sudden drop in blood pressure. It can also be an early sign of pregnancy.

The friends thou hast
And their adoption tried
Grapple them to thy soul
With hooks of steel.
(Shakespeare)
1926

The road to a friend's house is
    never long.
1920s

The thoughts of love are long, long thoughts
But memories sweet are longer
The bonds of wealth are strong, strong bonds
But friendship's ties are stronger
1928

There are gold ships
And silver ships
But the best ship
Is friendship.
1930s

There is a little word
In every language dear
In English tis Forget-Me-Not
In French tis Souvenir.
1920s

Things there are time cannot sever
And the long years cannot end

61

Love and faith will last for ever
In the bosom of a friend
1919

Two's company. Three's none.
Four's alright, if two walk on.
1920s

This album is one of friendship's dearest minions. It is the declared enemy of oblivion. Its owner may well regard it as of inestimable value.
1800s

This book beneath my hand that lies
Doth for its happy owner, hold
A treasure dearer far than gold
In its rich store of memories.
For writ within its pages fair
Are names which oft recall some place
Some sunny hour, some smiling face
Of those whose hands inscribed them there.
1920s

Whenever you see my message
Know I still think of you
Time may speed and pass for ever
But my friendship's always true
1951

We make new friends day by day
We laugh with them and jest
But when it comes to the uphill way
The old friends are the best
1937

THE TOILET.

When the summer sun is setting
And your mind from cares is free
When of absent friends you're thinking
Will you think of me.
1904

> *The intense red, pink and orange hues of the sky at sunset are mainly caused by scattering of sunlight by dust particles, soot particles and similar particles in the Earth's atmosphere.*

When months and years have glided by
And on this page you cast your eye
Remember t'was a friend sincere
Who wrote this kindly message here
1930s

When on a lonely path you've got
And may perchance you see
That little flower Forget-me-not,
Pluck it and think of me.
1920s

When this you see, remember me
And bear me in your mind.

Let all the world say what they will,
Speak of me as you find.
1922

Where 'ere you are
Where 'ere you be
Let me say
Remember me
1930s

Your album is a garden
That only friends may know
I will plant a forget-me-not
And see if it will grow
1900s

Your album is your garden plot
Where all your friends may sow
Where thorn and thistles flourish not
And naught but flowers grow.
I too within your garden plot
Would plant one seed
'Forget-Me-Not'
1920

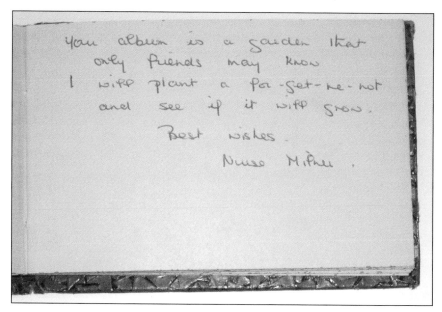

> *Among the many legends of the forget-me-not is one which says that the Christ child was sitting on Mary's lap and stated that he wished future generations could see her eyes. He touched them and then waved his hand over the ground and blue flowers appeared. They were called 'forget-me-not' to remind people of the beautiful blue colour of her eyes.*

Homily

A great sorrow will teach great truths
It will evaluate, emulate and subdue
Yet how its footsteps will sear and burn
The green garden of a fair soul.
1904

All common things, each day's events
That with the hour begin and end
Our pleasures and our discontents
Are bounds by which we may ascend
1910s

And when the great creator
Shall write against your name
It will not be have you won or lost
But how you played the game
(Grantland Rice)
1938

Ashes to Ashes
Dust to Dust
If God won't have you
The Devil must.
1920s

Blessed is the man who expected not
For he shall never be deceived
1928

Everything in the world is cut diamond-wise. It reflects in all directions.
1916

> *Diamonds are made completely of carbon, and the atoms form in such a way as to create the hardest known substance. This superior structure means that diamonds can be highly polished and appear more brilliant than any natural colourless gemstone.*

For gold the merchant ploughs the main
The farmer ploughs the manor
But glory is the soldier's prize.
The soldier's wealth is honour.
So poor, brave soldier, ne'er despise him
Nor count him as a stranger
Remember he's his country's stay
In day and hour of danger.
1920s

Four things a man must learn to do
If he would keep his record true
To think without confusion clearly
To love his fellow man sincerely
To act from honest motives purely
To trust in God and heaven securely.
1935

I shall pass through this world but once. Any good thing therefore that I can do, or any kindness that I can show to you, or yours, let me do it now – Let me not defer it, or neglect it, for I shall not pass this way again.
1925

If one looks on the bright side
'T will sure to be the right side
At least that's how I've found it
As I've journeyed through each day
And it's queer how shadows vanish
And how easy 't is to banish
From a bright side sort of nature
Every doleful thing away.
1908

If you know the truth and do it, the universe itself seconds you, and bears you on to sure victory everywhere.
(Carlyle)
1935

Life is mainly froth and bubble
Two things stand like stone
Kindness in another's trouble
Courage in our own.
(Lindsay Gordon)
1917

Life is a town of crooked streets
Death is the market place
Where all men meet
If life was a thing that money could buy
The rich would live
And the poor would die
1929

The painting of Bubbles by Sir John Millais became famous when it was used over many generations in advertisements for Pears soap during the nineteenth century. It depicts a boy with a bubble pipe and was modelled by Millais' five-year-old grandson William Milbourne James, who later rose to the rank of Admiral in the British navy but was known as 'Bubbles' for the rest of his life.

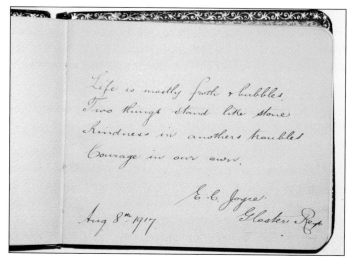

Life is mostly froth & bubbles
Two things stand like stone
Kindness in another's troubles
Courage in our own.

E. C. Joyce.
Gloster Rgt

Aug 8th 1917.

Money is like manure
No use when it is spread
1928

No matter how beautiful the human form,
At its best it is but a perishing thing.
1904

Oh! Better far to climb the toilsome height,
Than linger in the valley's flowered way;
Far Better in a losing cause to fight
Than feel one's sinews wasting day by day -
To taste the hemlock bitter, face the night,
Than die this daily death of apathy.
1910

Oh ye who complain of the grind
Remember these words (which are true!)
The dreariest job one can find
Is looking for something to do.
(Walt Whitman)
1920

Success is a journey, not a destination.
1930s

The easy path in the lowland hath little of grand or new
But a toilsome ascent leads on to a wide and glorious view
Peopled and warm is the valley; lonely and chill is the height
But the peak that is nearer the storm cloud is nearer the stars of light.
1930s

The Lord watch between me and thee while we are absent one from another.
1920s

> This phrase comes from the story of Jacob and his father-in-law in the Old Testament book of Genesis, and is known as the 'Mizpah' benediction.

The only place where success comes before work is in the dictionary.
1930s

Then welcome each rebuff
That turns earth's smoothness rough
Each sting that bids nor sit nor stand but go!
Be our joys three-parts pain
Strive, and hold cheap the strain
Learn, nor account the pang; dare, never grudge the throe!
Be the fire ashes, what survives is gold.
(Robert Browning)
1916

To catch Dame Fortune's golden smile,
Assiduous wait upon her,
And gather gear by every wile
That's justified by honour,
Not for to hide it in a hedge,
Nor for the glorious privilege,
Of being independent.
(R.Burns)
1900s

> 'Dame Fortune', Fortuna, was the personification of luck, both good
> luck and bad luck, in the religion of Ancient Rome.

To every man there openeth a way and ways and a way
And the High Soul climbs the High Way
And the Low Soul gropes the Low
And in between, on the misty flats
The rest drift to and fro;
But to every man there openeth a High Way and a Low
And every man decideth
The way his soul shall go.
(John Oxenham)
1926

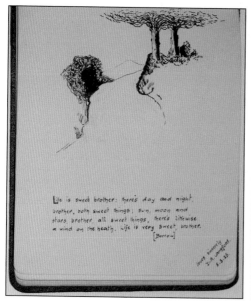

The world is so full of a number of things
I'm sure that we all should be happy as kings
(R L Stevenson)
1934

True happiness
Consists not in the multitude of friends
But in the worth and choice
(Ben Jonson)
1904

We can better help another by fanning a glimmer of goodness than
by censuring his faults.
(Edmund Gibson)
1916

We say it for an hour or for years
We say it smiling, say it choked with tears
We say it coldly, say it with a kiss
And yet we have no other word other than this, 'Goodbye'.

We have no dearer word for our hearts friend,
For him who journeys to the world's far end,
And sears our soul with going; thus we say,
As unto him who steps but o'er the way, 'Goodbye'

Alike to those we love and those we hate
We say no more in parting at life's gate,
To him who passes out beyond earth's sight
We cry, as to the wanderer for the night, 'Goodbye'.
(Charles Dickens)
1906

We should conceal our weakness before the strong.
1916

Love and Kisses

A kiss is a peculiar thing
Of use to no-one but absolute bliss to two.
The small boy gets it for nothing
Whist the young man has to steal it
'Tis a baby's right, a lover's privilege
And an old man's purchase

71

To a young maid it means faith
To a married woman, hope
And to an old maid – charity.
1908

> The word 'kiss' derives from the Old English *cyssan* 'to kiss'. Although
> kissing is a common expression of affection among people, until modern
> times it was unknown to certain cultures, including many African tribes.

Cats like mice
Mice like cheese
Girls like boys
Boys like these
X X X X X X
1953

Cupid and my Campaspe play'd
At cards for kisses: Cupid paid.
He stakes his quiver, bow, and arrows,
His mother's doves, and team of sparrows:
Loses them too. Then down he throws
The coral of his lip, the rose
Growing on one's cheek (but none knows how);
With these, the crystal of his brow,
And then the dimple on his chin:
All these did my Campaspe win.
At last he set her both his eyes:
She won, and Cupid blind did rise.
(J. Lyly)
1900s

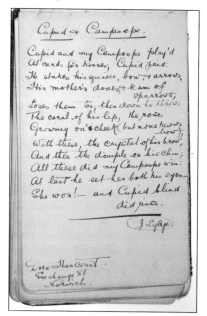

God bless thee T'is the fondest wish
A mother's heart can give
What worlds of loving tenderness
In these sweet words as live.
1922

Hair was made to crimp and curl
Cheeks were made to blush
Eyes were made to rove about
Lips were made to (Oh Hush)
1908

If a girl gets a kiss
And goes and tells her mother
She ought to be an old maid
And never get another
1928

If you love me
As I love you,
No knife could cut
Our love in two
1880s

Kisses are sweet
When two lips meet
But oh so dry
On paper
1931

A BIG SECRET.

My love to all those that I love
My love to all those that love me
My love those that love those that I love
And to those that love those that love me.
1908

The Art of Kissing:

Most people kiss but not one in a hundred knows how to extract
Bliss from the lovely lips any more than he knows how to extract
demands. When going to kiss never kiss anyone on any other part
than the lips. The gentleman should be a bit taller than the Lady. He
should have clean face, and mouth full of expression. Take the left
hand of the Lady in your right and place your left on her shoulder
then let it gently fall to her side. Do not hurry; gently and lovingly
draw her heart to your heart. Her head will fall on your shoulder
which will cause your heart to flutter. Do not hurry, when you are
nearly heart to heart and do not squeeze her. Look into her eyes
gently and manly press her to your breast, now stand firm and do
not shiver. Now her lips are open take good aim and press your lips
to hers, do not take your lips away at once but press them well
together. Your nerves will dance before you and you will think you are
in H——-???? Now the art of kissing is learnt it requires nothing but

love to make it perfect. Always respect the girl you kiss and do not
kiss if you cannot kiss properly.
'By Shakespeare'.

*(The sender of this piece writes, 'This is a real oddity. It's written over
the last two pages of the book, not signed or initialled and was written
in the book of a married woman (although her husband had deserted
her and disappeared by this time). Still, it seems a little bit risqué. In
fact I'm surprised at how much writing about kissing and men and
women was in this 1920s album. They seem to have been as obsessed
by it as we are now! I very much doubt that it really was written by
Shakespeare, but I could be wrong about that. It seems like an excuse to
me – it must be OK because it's Shakespeare!')*

What's a home without a mother?
What's a man without a miss?
What's a maid without a lover?
What's a hug without a kiss?
1909

Pastoral

A thing of beauty is a joy forever
(J. Keats)
*(This was written in my autograph book by the headmaster of my Junior
School in the 1950s. He drew a picture of a landscape with a rabbit as
well!)*

All thoughts that are pure, Unselfish and bright,
Shall flourish as flowers, In sweet summer light,
And send out their magic, To banish all fears,
Bring sunlight to eyes, So dim with sad tears.
1920s

Any old fish can swim down the stream, but it takes a live one to
swim up.
1919

Face the sun and you cannot see the shadow
*(This was written in my autograph book by my teacher at my Junior
School in the 1950s)*

Happy is the day
That the sun shines on
1900

Here with a loaf of bread
Beneath the bough, a book
A verse a flush of wine and
Thou singing to me in the wilderness,
And wilderness is paradise now.
1918

Island of Dreams
It lies in the deep where the blue water
    gleams
A beautiful island, an island of dreams
Where sweet tender faces flit to and fro
The loves that we lov'd in the dear long ago
And our hearts they must beat and our
    burning tears fall
As we see their hands waving and hear their lips call
Oh island of dreams, oh star of the deep
I am weeping and waiting and longing to sleep

But there far away from the world and its pain
I meet you my darling, I hold you again
And we tread the old paths as in days that have been
With no one to part us, no shadow between
And I feel your heart beating; I see your eyes shine
And dreaming or waking I know you are mine
Oh island of dreams, oh star of the deep
I am weeping and waiting and longing to sleep.
1906

Kind hearts are the gardens.
Kind thoughts are the roots.
Kind words are the blossoms.
Kind deeds are the fruits
Love is the sweetest sunshine
That warms into life.
For only in darkness
Grow hatred and strife.
1920

> *The Roman conquerors of Britain planted ornamental gardens in Britain in the first century AD. Many of the plants which they introduced are still cultivated in Britain today.*

Keep your face turned towards the sun and then shadows will fall behind.
1916

Sunset
The golden sea its mirror spreads
Beneath the golden skies,
And but a narrow strip between of land and shadow lies
1920s

The song of the birds for pardon
The kiss of the sun for mirth
You are nearer to God in a garden
Than any place else on Earth.
1940s

The year's at the spring,
And day's at the morn;
Morning's at seven;
The hill-side's dew-pearled;

The lark's on the wing;
The snail's on the thorn;
God's in his Heaven -
All's right with the world!
(Robert Browning)
1904

There is a town in Kentucky, America, called Pippa Passes, named after the poem by Robert Browning, from which the above extract is taken.

Thy voiceless lips o' flowers
Are living preachers
Each cup a pulpit
And each leaf a book;
Supplying to my memory
Numerous preachers
In loneliest nook
(Horatio Smith)
1909

When the golden sun is setting
And your mind from care is free
When of others you are thinking
Will you sometimes think of me?
1890

Where do the little blue violets grow?
In the cleft of the lonely hill
Sheltered safe from the sun's hot glow
And the touch of the breezes chill.

The sorrowful soul may find them there,
The eyes that are weary, know
There is tender comfort and rest from care
Where the little violets grow.
1919

There are around 400 species of violet/viola. The twelve varieties found growing wild in Britain include the dog violet, the sweet violet, the fen violet and the dame's violet.

Wishes and Blessings

A long life and a happy one, a tall man and a good one.
1927

Dear daughter, Here's hoping that you will always be a good
obedient daughter to me.
1927

Does anyone know, does anyone care?
Where you go or how you fare,
Whether you smile, or whether you sigh
Whether you laugh or whether you cry,
Glad when you are happy,
Sad when you are blue,
Does anyone care what becomes of you?
I'll say I do!
1930s

I care not much for gold or land;
Give me a mortgage here and there,
Some good bank stock – some note of hand,
Or trifling railroad share;

I only ask that Fortune send
A little *more* than I shall spend'
1920

I will not wish thee grandeur,
I will not wish thee wealth
Only a contented mind,
Peace, competence, and health,
Fond friends to love thee dearly,
And honest ones to chide
And faithful ones to cleave to thee,
Whatever may betide.
1910

I wish you health
I wish you wealth
I wish you gold in store
I wish you heaven when you die
What can I wish you more?
1920s

If I had a fairy's might
I'd rule the earth both day and night
I'd quickly put the people right
And make their money fly
My maxim should be fair and square
Every man should have his share
The rich would have the pudding
And the poor would have the pie.
1906

If I knew the box where the smiles are kept
No matter how large the key
Or strong the bolt, I would try so hard
It would open, I know, for me
Then over the land and the sea broadcast
I'd scatter the smiles to play
That the children's faces might hold them fast
For many and many a day

If I knew a box that was large enough
To hold all the frowns I meet
I would like to gather them every one

79

From nursery school and street
Then folding and holding I'd pack them in
And turn the monster key
I'd hire a giant to drop the box
To the depths of the deep, deep sea.
1907

Just wealth enough to free from care
Just health enough to stand life's wear
Just friends enough faithful and true
To make life's path a joy to you.
1926

May health and happiness wealth and joy
To whom this book belongs enjoy
And may all friends who write in this
Have all the pleasures that they wish
1906

May there be just enough cloud in your life to make a glorious
sunset.
1930

May you live as long as you want
But may you never want as long as you live.
1922

May your joys be as long as a bunny's ears
And your sorrows as short as his tail.
1950s

In the wild, rabbits are prey, not predators, so they must always be on guard. This is why their ears are so long and can be used independently to listen in different directions. Their white tails are called 'scuts', and are used to warn other rabbits of a predator.

May your life be like arithmetic:
Your joys added,
Your cares subtracted,
Your happiness multiplied,
And your sorrows divided.
1950s

To you, dear friend,
One wish I give
That you may be happy
As long as you live.
1920s

What shall I wish thee young friend of mine,
Plenty of peace, and calm and wine,
These if Gods will, but thine be grace,
The sunshine of thy saviour's face,
The shelter of his hands.
1908

Where ere you go
What ere you do
Whichever path you tread
May love divine and friendship true
Shower blessings on your head
1906

CHAPTER FOUR

Popular favourites and interesting entries from over the decades

SOME RHYMES SEEM to crop up time and again. They can be found in Victorian autograph albums and albums from the 1950s and 1960s. These are verses or quotes which have for one reason or another, captured the imagination and been passed down through the generations.

At my primary school in the 1950s it seemed essential to inscribe the following inside the front cover of your autograph book:

If this book should dare to roam
Box its ears and send it home

You would then list your address as follows, with as many entries as you could come up with, including:

House number
Street
Town
City
Country
Continent
Earth
Space
Universe

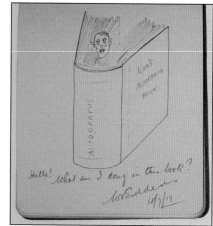

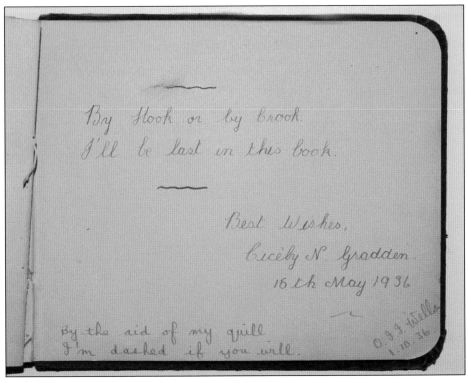

By hook or by crook and other album comments

By hook or by crook
I'll be first in this book.
1900s

By the aid of my quill
I'm dashed if you will
1930s

By hook or by crook
I'll be last in this book.
1918

By egg or by bacon
I think you're mistaken
1950s

To beat the other
I'll write on the cover.
1924

Not so fast.
I'm the last!
1930s

There are several theories as to the origin of the phrase 'By hook or by crook'. One which seems quite plausible, relates to a medieval English custom of allowing peasants to gather dead wood from the royal forests by pulling it with a shepherd's crook or gathering it with a billhook.

Hey Diddle Diddle
I am in the middle
(Written across the middle pages of an autograph book)
1920s

Can't think,	Head weak
Brain numb,	Brain dumb
Inspiration won't come,	Inspiration won't come
Can't write,	Can't write
Bad pen,	Bad pen
Much love,	That's all
Amen	Amen
1940s	*1935*

This is my album but learn ere you look
That all are expected to add to my book
You are welcome to quiz
But the penalty is
You must fill up a page
For others to quiz
1900s

I will start at the beginning
Goodness knows who will fill the end
This will carry all
The wishes of a friend
1910

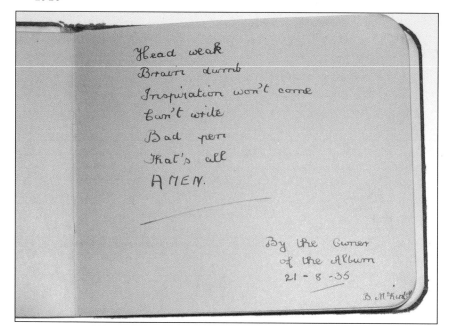

I've looked these pages o'er and o'er
To see what others wrote before,
And in this little lovely spot,
I'll here inscribe forget me not.
1888

What, write in a book
At which ladies will look?
Not I. I'm Shy. Goodbye.
1902

What, write in this book
For critics to look
And gentlemen to spy?
Not I, Not I!
1907

I have the book
I have the pen
I don't know what to write
So I will just inscribe my name
And trust that that's alright.
1920s

If writing in Albums
True Friendship Ensures
With the greatest of pleasure
I'll scribble in Yours
1920s

The owner of this book has asked
A word or two from me
But being in a generous mood
I've written twenty-three.
1936

On this page
Pure and white
Only a friend
Would dare to write
1921

Some to you have written
Some to you may write
But none thinks of you more Truly
Than the one who writes these
lines tonight.
1922

I've been asked to write in your album
I don't know how to begin
There's nothing original in me
Except the original sin.
1936

When I took up this book to write
I found a page all clean and white
I thought and thought and thought in vain
And then I thought I'd write my name.
1919

I've been asked to write in your album I don't know how to begin, There's nothing original in me Except the "Original Sin".

Olive J. J. Wells.
2nd October 1936.

> Original sin is a Christian doctrine; a belief that everyone is born sinful. Even newborn babies have it in them – born with a built-in urge to do wrong and to disobey God.

Your life is too nice to be blank like this page
1933

I'll write on pink
To save the ink
And leave the yellow
For your fellow.
1930s

I'm writing on this page of pink
But what to write I cannot think
To spoil this page I think a shame
So I just think I'll sign my name
1930s

Variations on a theme

I'm writing on this page of blue
But don't know what to write for you
To spoil this page I think a shame
So I just think I'll sign my name.
1953

I'm writing on this page of green
To show I hold you in esteem
To spoil this page I think a shame
So I just think I'll sign my name.
1930s

I'm writing on this page of gold
Though unsure if I'm too bold
To spoil this page I think a shame
So I just think I'll sign my name.
1936

Usually the pages of autograph books are pastel shades of pink, green blue and lemon, hence the colour references.

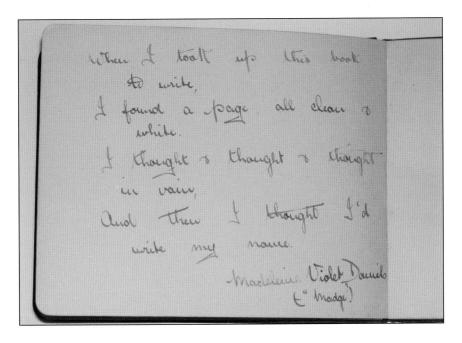

Last in this book I've chosen to be
But, last in your thoughts
Would be great pain to me.
1919

Flowers

I'm not an English beauty,
I'm not an English rose,
I'm just a little schoolgirl,
With freckles on her nose.
1955

Little deeds like little seeds
Grow and grow and grow
Some are flowers and some are weeds
Giving joy and woe
Let us sow but happy deeds
Everywhere we go
1935

Little seeds like little deeds
Grow to flowers
Or else to weeds.
1930s

Roses are red
Violets are blue
Sugar is sweet
And so are you
1922

Roses are red,
Violets are blue,
Beyond the horizon
Are riches for you.
1932

The most famous garden rose of all time is the 'Peace Rose', a hybrid tea with large light yellow and cream-coloured flowers. It was developed immediately before the Second World War by French horticulturist Francis Meilland and was given its name after the war, when it was released for sale.

Roses are red
Violets are blue
You don't know me
And I don't know you
1937

Roses are red
Violets are blue
I'm not sweet
Neither are you
1950s

Roses are red,
Violets are blue
I was born lovely
What happened to you?
1952

Roses are red
Violets are blue
All these flowers
I give to you
1930s

The words 'She bathed with roses red, and violets blue, And all the sweetest flowers, that in the forest grew' were written by Edmund Spenser in his epic poem 'The Faerie Queene' in 1590.

Roses are red
Violets are blue
Pinks are sweet
And so are you
1922

Roses are red
Violets are blue
Portsmouth 5
Stanley 2
(Cup tie 1925)
1928

The song 'Roses are Red, My Love, Violets are Blue' was a hit for American singer Bobby Vinton in 1962. It told of a verse written in a year book on graduation day.

Roses are red
Pansies are blue
Lilies are lovely
And so are you
1950s

Roses are blue
Daffodils grey
It all sounds wrong
Still, Never mind, eh!
1950s

Roses may wither
Leaves may die
Friends may forget you
But never will I.
1930s

Rose of the Garden,
Such is woman's lot
Worshipped while blooming
When she fades, forgot.
1910

Tulips, or two lips, which are the best.
I prefer the two lips, must be confessed.
Tulips are pretty pleasing to the eye
But two lips well pressed, will electrify.
1920s

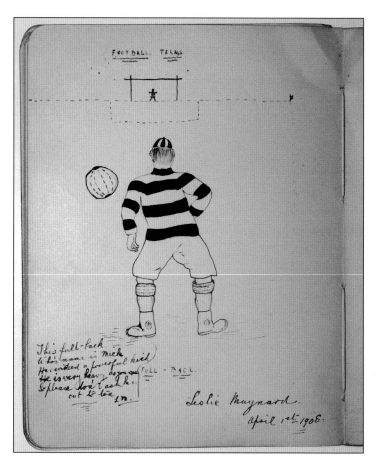

Tulips in the garden
Tulips in the park,
The two lips that (name) likes best,
Are (name) in the dark
1960s
(*This rhyme requires the insertion of a girl's name and a boy's name*)

Underneath the mistletoe
Underneath the rose
But the proper place for kissing
Is underneath the nose
1920s

> *According to tradition, Druid priests prized mistletoe in medicine and also as a symbol of peace. They used a golden sickle to harvest it, and would never let it touch the ground.*

Love and Babies

Don't kiss at the garden gate
Love is blind but neighbours ain't
1950s

Kissing don't last,
  cooking do.
1940s

(First name) for now
(First name) for ever
(Maiden name) for now
But not for ever.
1950s

(First name) is my Name
Single is my station
Happy be the gentleman
That makes the alteration
1920s

Hearts when you're in love,
Diamonds when you're engaged,
Clubs when you're married,
Spades when you're grave
1950s

I love you
I love you
I love you, I do.
But don't get excited
I love monkeys too.
1960s

I love you on the hilltop,
I love you on the level
And when I get you in my arms
I love you like the devil.
1960s

It's hard to part from those we love
When our hearts are full of hope.
And harder yet to find the towel
When our eyes are full of soap.
1950s

Love is blind
Love is crazy
Love is pulling petals
Off a daisy.
1950s

Repeating the phrase 'He loves me, he loves me not' as the petals are pulled from a daisy reveals whether or not a lover is true – and it all depends whether the final petal is a 'love' or a 'love me not'. If a girl throws the golden centre of a daisy into the air, the number of pieces which fall onto her hand reveal the number of children she will have. The daisy derived its English name from the term 'day's eye', which referred to the way the flower opens and closes with the sun.

May you be happy,
And live at your ease,
And have a good husband,
To scold when you please
1900s

O woman! in our hours of ease,
Uncertain, coy, and hard to please,
But, barring pins, how soft to squeeze.
Spokesheare.

May your husband be sweet
And your house be neat
And on the floor
Some tiny feet.
1920s

Remember me on the river
Remember me on the lake
Remember me on your wedding day
And give me a piece of cake.
1950s

Needles and pins
Needles and pins
When you get married
Your trouble begins
1960s

It is unlucky if a bride and groom meet on the wedding day before the service and she should never wear her complete wedding outfit before the day. To ensure good luck the bride should wear something old, something new, something borrowed and something blue.

There's water in the ocean
There's water in the sea.
And when you have a baby,
There'll be water on your knee
1940s

When you get married and have twins
Don't come to me for safety pins.
1950s

When (name) was a little girl
It was toys, toys, toys
Now (name) is a big girl
It's boys, boys, boys.
1950s

In the UK about one in thirty-four babies is born a twin. Up to forty per cent of twins develop a twin language, 'idioglossia', often known as the secret language of twins.

When you get married
And live by the river
I'll kill my old cow
And give you the liver
1950s

When you get married
And life gets too hard
I'll lend you my shovel
To dig up the yard.
1930s

When you get married
And live in a house
I'll buy you a cat
To catch the mouse.
1950s

When you get married
And get very poor
I'll post bread and cheese
And apples through your door.
1950s

When your husband is angry
And raging and cross
Pick up the poker
And show him who's boss.
1950s

When your husband is thirsty
And asks for a drink
Go to the kitchen
And show him the sink
1960s

Brides in ancient Rome wore a girdle fastened with many tiny knots which the groom had to untie before he could bed his new wife.

When you get married,
And your husband gets cross,
Take up a poker,
And show him who's boss.
1960s

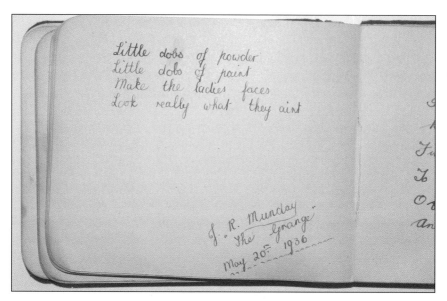

Little dobs of powder
Little dobs of paint
Make the ladies faces
Look really what they aint

J. R. Munday
"The Grange"
May 20th 1936

When you have babies
Who fret and cry
Will I look after them?
No, not I!
1930s

When you have babies
One, two, three
Please don't think
You can give them to me.
1950s

When you grow old
And just can't bend
Call on me
To be your friend
1960s

Powder, paint and preening

Fiery temper it is said
Smoulders hot in tresses red
But there are people who admit
They like a nice hot time of it
1900s

Happiness is a kind of perfume
which cannot be shed on others
without catching a few drops
oneself.
1931

Hide and Seek.
E. Wright
21-10-31

Little dobs of powder
Little dobs of paint
Make the ladies faces
Look really what they ain't.
1936

Little puffs of powder
Little dabs of paint
Make a girls complexion
Look like what it ain't
1950s

Little drops of water
Added to the milk
Lets the milkman's daughter
Dress herself in silk.
1950s

This one rather implies that the milkman's daughter (or, more probably, the milkman himself, was watering down his products!

Our troubles come,
From trying to put
The left-hand shoe
On the right-hand foot.
1909

She was the fairest maid of all
In Somerset and Dorset
Her little heart
Went pit-a-pat
Beneath the whalebone corset.
1909

When you get old and cannot see
Put on your specs and think of me.
1950s

Silly Chants

(Name) and a monkey were sitting on a rail,
You wouldn't know the difference if (name) had a tail
1960s

I sent a message to heaven
To say I was ready to die
The answer came back
You can sit on a tack
And wait till the clouds roll by
1930

If all the boys lived over the
    sea
What a good swimmer
    (name) would be
1960s

If in heaven we don't meet
Hand in hand we'll stand the heat
And if it gets intensely hot
Pepsi Cola hits the spot!
1960s

Matilda had jam
Matilda had jelly
Matilda went home
With a pain in her —-
Now don't be mistaken
Now don't be misled
Matilda went home
With a pain in her head.
1931

> *Yet another of those 'pious' rhymes which use a line to disguise a slightly rude word – in this case 'belly'*

My brother is a good boy
He goes to church on Sunday
To ask dear God to give him strength
To fight the lads on Monday
1940s

My sister is a good girl
She goes to church on Sunday
And prays to God to give her strength
To kiss the boys on Monday
1950s

My teacher is a holy man
He goes to church on
Sunday
He prays to God to give
him strength
To cane the boys on
Monday
1940s

Shine like a glow worm,
A glow worm's never glum
'Cos how can you be grumpy
When the sun shines out your bum?
1960s

> *The glow worm is not a worm but a small beetle. Only the wingless females glow to attract the flying males. Each female has an adult glowing life of just a few weeks and dies soon after her eggs are laid.*

(Name, name) sits in the tub
Mother forgot to put in the plug
Oh my goodness, oh my soul
There goes (name) down the hole
1940s

Remember the good old school days
When you and I were young.
We used to pull each other's hair
And chew each other's gum.
1950s

Remember the girl from the city,
Remember the girl from the town.
Remember the girl who ruined your book
By writing upside down
1930s
(Written upside down in the autograph book)

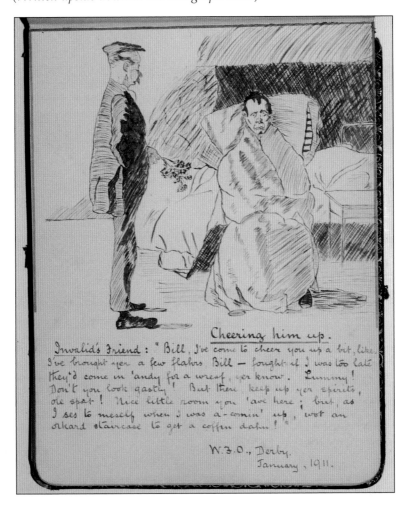

Cheering him up.

Invalid's Friend : " Bill, I've come to cheer you up a bit, like.
I've brought yer a few flahrs Bill — fought if I was too late
they'd come in 'andy for a wreaf, yer know. Lummy!
Don't you look gasty! But there keep up yer spirits,
ole spat! Nice little room you 'ave here; but, as
I ses to meself when I was a-comin' up, wot an
orkard staircase to get a coffin dahn!"

W.3.O., Derby.
January, 1911.

CHAPTER FIVE

Tongue twisters and clever rhymes

FROM LIMERICKS THROUGH to word play, the variety of witty inscriptions found in autograph books is infinite. This is just a selection from those I have come across.

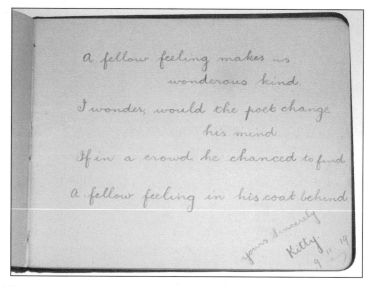

A fellow feeling makes us wondrous kind
I wonder, would the poet change his mind
If in a crowd he chanced to find
A fellow feeling in his coat behind.
1919

A fire broke out in the middle of the ocean.
The blind man saw it, the deaf man heard it.
The man with no legs ran for the fire engine.
The fire engine came with two dead horses.
The two dead horses ran over two dead cats
And half killed them
1920s

A silly boy was Jimmy Stout
He dived off the pier
When the tide had gone out
1935

A wise old owl sat on an oak
The more he saw the less he spoke.
The less he spoke the more he heard
I wish more people were like that bird!
1930s

> *Tawny Owls are Britain's largest and most common owl and have the distinctive hoot 'tu wit tu woo'. Their exceptionally large eyes give them good night vision.*

A tutor who tooted the flute
Tried to tutor two tooters to toot

A wise old owl lived in an oak;
The more he thought, the less he spoke,
The less he spoke, the more he heard,
Why aren't we like that old bird?
H. M. Bayley.
3.10.35

Said the two to the tutor
Is it harder to toot
Or to tutor two tooters to toot?
1900s

Adam and Eve and Pinchme
Went down to the river to bathe
Adam and Eve were drowned
Who do you think was saved?
Answer: Pinch me (a pinch was then administered when the rhyme was read out)
1930s

Algy met a bear
The bear met Algy
The bear was bulgy
The bulge was Algy.
My grandfather wrote this in my autograph book in the 1950s

Betty bought butter but the
butter was too bitter
So Betty bought better butter to
make the bitter butter better
1940s

Parody:
Eat well, sweet maid;
And let who will be slender.
Eat and grow fat
No matter how you feel.
And make through life
On food both good and tender
One long, sweet meal.
1907

This is a parody on a poem called 'A Farewell' by Charles Kingsley in which the second verse begins 'Be good, sweet maid, and let who will be clever.' (See also Chapter 2).

Eating more than he was able
Johnny died at the breakfast table

'If you please'
Said little Meg
'May I have his other egg?'
1930s

Everyone knows Mary Rose
But nobody knows Mary Rose
Sat on a pin –
Mary Rose
Written in my daughter's book
by her grandfather 1980s

Far and few, far and few
Are the lands where the jumblies live
Their heads are green and their hands are blue
And they went to sea in a sieve, they did
They went to see in a sieve.
(*Edward Lear*)
1940s

He sifted a peck of unsifted thistles
He unsifted a peck of sifted thistles
Did Theophilus Thwaites
The thistle sifter
1919

I don't give a jot
What any poet said
Be it ever so humble
There's no place like bed.
1918

I saw a house
'Twas out of sight
A million miles away
The sun shone on it brilliantly
About the break of day
Its doors propelled backwards
Its front was at the back
Alone it stood amongst all others
And it was whitewashed. Black
1930s

I went to the pictures tomorrow,
I took a front row in the back,
I fell from the pit to the gallery,
And broke a front bone in my back
I went round a straight crooked corner
And saw a dead donkey alive
I took out my pistol to stab him
And he landed me one in the eye.
1930s

I went to the pictures tomorrow;
I got a front seat at the back.
A lady gave me an orange;
I ate it, and gave it her back.
1930s

No one person can be said to have invented cinema, but in 1893 the Edison company successfully demonstrated the Kinetoscope, enabling one viewer at a time to see the moving pictures. In 1885 the Lumière brothers were the first to present projected, moving photographic pictures to a paying audience.

Parody on Kingsley's Poem

Eat well, sweet maid;
And let who will be slender:
Eat & grow fat;
No matter how you feel;
And make, through life,
On food both good & tender,
One long sweet meal

Eileen Avarne

Sep^t 17th 1907

PLAYTIME.

105

If all the world was paper
And all the sea was ink
And all the trees were bread and cheese
What would we have to drink?
1920s

In days of old
When knights were bold
And suits were made of tin
No mortal cry
Escaped the guy
Who sat upon a pin.
1930s

It isn't the miss in the engine
That causes the trouble, by heck.
It's the Miss beside the driver
With her arms around his neck.
1950s

> *George Stephenson tested his locomotive 'Blucher' on the Cillingwood Railway in July 1814 and the first person to patent a passenger road locomotive was Julius Griffiths in 1821. The famous locomotive the 'Rocket' was entered for the Rainhill Trials in October 1829 by Robert Stephenson.*

Never trouble trouble
Till trouble troubles you
It only doubles trouble
And troubles others too.
1936

Owen Moore went out one day
Owing more than he could pay
Owen Moore came back next day
Owing More
1919

Said the shoe to the sock
I'll make a hole in you
Said the sock to the shoe
I'll be darned if you do.
1936

> *The earliest shoes were made from large leaves, bark and grass, and tied on to the foot with vines. In hot lands these developed into sandals woven from palm leaves or grass, and in colder lands shoes, such as moccasins, were made from animal skins.*

The elephant is a bonnie bird.
It flits from bough to bough.
It makes its nest in a rhubarb tree
And whistles like a cow
1960s

The lightning flashed
The thunder crashed
The whole wide world was shaken
A little pig curled up its tail
And ran to save his bacon
1930s

There was a young fellow called Fred
Who fell from the wrong side of bed
He thought it was funny
To land on his tummy
With his feet in the place of his head
1940s

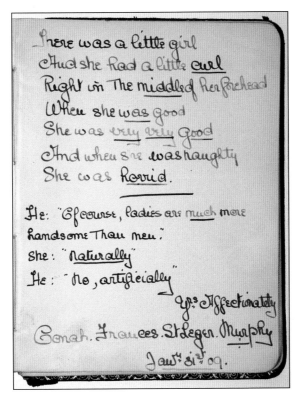

There was a little girl
And she had a little curl
Right in the middle of her forehead
When she was good
She was very very good
And when she was naughty
She was horrid.

He: "Of course, ladies are much more
handsome than men."
She: "Naturally"
He: "No, artificially"

Yrs Affectionately
Sonah. Frances. St Leger. Murphy
Jan 31st 09.

There was a little girl
And she had a little curl
Right in the middle of her forehead
When she was good, she was very very good
But when she was bad, she was horrid.
1909

There was a tom cat sat on our back wall
'Is feet was covered with blisters
'Is head went up, 'is tail went down
And the wind blew through 'is whiskers
1910

You may talk of the joys of summer
Of the birds you may often sing
But sitting down on a sharp tin-tack
Is the sign of an early spring
1920

When I was going to St Ives
I met a man with seven wives
Each wife had seven sacks
Each sack had seven cats
Each cat had seven kits
Kits, cats, sacks and wives
How many were there going to St Ives?
Answer: None (*They must have been coming from St Ives if the poet had met them. Unless, of course, they met at a cross roads!*)
1917

There was an old man from Perth
Who was born on the day of his birth
He was married they say on his wife's wedding day
And died on his last day on earth
1920s

Whether the weather be hot
Or whether the weather be cold
We'll whether the weather
Whatever the weather
Whether we like it or not.
1934

Willy in his new blue sashes
Fell in the fire and was burned to ashes
Although the room is getting chilly
We haven't the heart to poke poor Willy.
1930s

Yesterday upon the stair
I met a man who wasn't there
He wasn't there again today
I wish that he would go away.
My father invariably wrote this in autograph books
1950s

You hit your brother with a chair
Why did you do it Mabel?
I did it said the little girl
Cos I couldn't lift the table.
1950s

Nursery rhymes and parodies

Elvis Presley banged his head
Elvis Presley went to bed
When Tommy Steele came along
He made him put a bandage on.
1950s

Presumably based on the rhythm of the nonsense rhyme 'Diddle diddle dumpling, my son John', this verse mentions two of the most popular singers of the day – Britain's Tommy Steele and America's Elvis Presley. Girls would usually be either 'Tommy fans' or 'Elvis fans'.

Humpty Dumpty sat on the wall
Humpty Dumpty had a great fall
All the kings' horses and all the kings' men
Had scrambled eggs for breakfast again
1960s

Humpty Dumpty was originally a large cannon. Centuries after the rhyme was written, Lewis Carroll used the name 'Humpty Dumpty' in his book 'Alice through the Looking Glass', depicting him as an egg. After that, the rhyme was believed to be about an egg, rather than a gun.

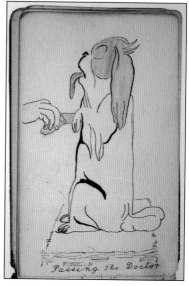

Passing The Doctor

Little Jack Horner sat in
    a corner,
Eating his Christmas pie.
He put in his thumb
And pulled out a plum
And the juice squirted up
in his eye
1950s

Little Jack Horner was reputed to have been the Steward to Richard Whiting, the Bishop of Glastonbury, during the reign of Henry VIII. The Bishop tried to bribe the King by sending a gift of twelve title deeds to various English manorial estates hidden in a pie to thwart thieves, and 'Jack' (actually Thomas) opened the pastry and extracted one deed 'or plum' for himself.

Little Jack Horner sat in a corner,
Eating his mother's pie.
How did she do it?
Without any suet,
And fat as big as a fly.
1948

Jack and Jill went up the hill,
To get a pail of water.
Jill came down with half a
    crown.
It wasn't for the water.
1950s

This parody seems to have surfaced in the 1940s, and relates to the food shortages in Britain at the time.

Little Miss Muffet
Sat on a tuffet
Her drawers all tattered and torn
It wasn't a spider who sat down beside her
It was Little Boy Blue with his horn
1960s

Little Miss Muffet
Sat on a tuffet
Eating her curds and whey
Along came a spider
And sat down beside her
And she ate that as well.
1950s

Mary had a little watch
She swallowed it one day
And now she's taking Beecham's pills
To pass the time away.
1950s

Mary had a little hen,
Its ways were very queer,
It laid like mad when eggs were cheap,
And stopped when eggs were dear.
1970s

Mary had a little lamb
Its fleece was black as soot
And into Mary's bread and jam
It's sooty foot it put.
1950s

Mary had a little lamb
Its fleas were black and hairy
Its teeth were green, its eyes were red
It really looked quite scary
1970s

Mary had a little lamb
She tied it to a pylon
A 1,000 volts ran down its tail
And changed its fleece to nylon
1970s

Mary had a little lamb
The butcher killed it dead
Now she's taking it to school
Between two loaves of bread
1930s

The original nursery rhyme, 'Mary had a little Lamb' is American and was written by Sarah Hale of Boston in 1830. Interestingly it was chosen by Thomas Edison as the first rhyme to ever be recorded on his new invention, the phonograph.

Mary had a little lamb
She also had a bear
I've often seen her little lamb
But never seen her bare
1920s

Mary had a little lamb
The lamb was rather rude
One day it cut its fleece right off
And stood there in the nude
1950s

Three blind mice
Three blind mice
Elvis P is nice
Elvis P is nice
I hope that he will marry me
And give me babies 1, 2, 3
And you can take care of them all for me
Three blind mice
1959

Mary had a little lamb
Jack had a little less
And what she had for afterward
I'll leave you all to guess
1930s

> The original version of 'Three Blind Mice' is steeped in history and recounts the deaths of three clergymen, Ridley, Crammer and Latimer. They were ordered by Mary Tudor to be burnt at the stake in 1555 because they refused to renounce their Protestant faith. Mary Tudor (the 'farmer's wife' in the original) was a staunch Catholic and became nicknamed 'Bloody Mary' because of her violent persecution of Protestants. This parody of the rhyme celebrates the popularity of singer Elvis Presley, adored by schoolgirls in the 1950s.

In Disguise

If your B m t
Put:
If your B.
Putting:

(If your grate be empty
Put coal on
If your grate be full stop
Putting coal on)
1922

YY U R
YY U B
ICUR
YY
4 ME

2 good
2 b
4 got 10
(Too good to be forgotten)
1950s

YRU here?
What RU4?
Will UB there
When I close the door?

(Why are you here?
What are you for?
Will you be there
When I close the door?)
1960s

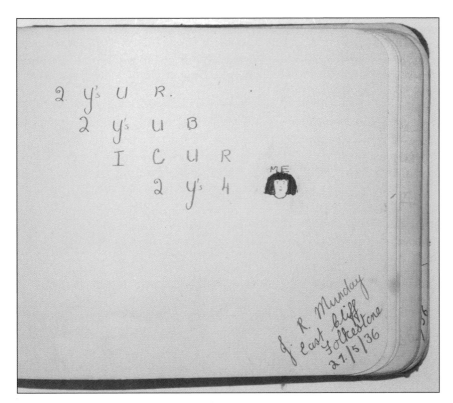

(Too wise you are
Too wise you be
I see you are
Too wise for me)
1950s

UROK
AX4U

(You are okay, a kiss for you)
1960s

O U Q T
I N V U

(Oh you cutie
I envy you)
1960s

URAQT

(You are a cutie)
1960s

2 young
+2 go
————
4 boys

(Too young to go for boys)
1950s

113

Down	and	you	and	find	you	you	will
And	you	love	you	I	love	for	be
Up	will	I	love	if	me	love	forgot!
Read	see	that	me	but	not	my	

(Read up and down and you will see that I love you and you love me, but if I find you love me not, my love for you will be forgot!)
1930s

Down	and	friend	that
And	you	a	friend
Up	will	have	is
Read	see	you	me

(Read up and down and you will see you have a friend that friend is me)
1930s

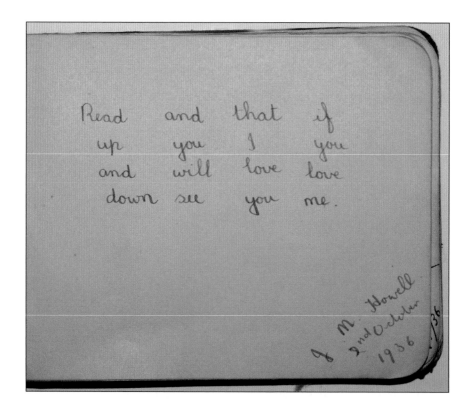

Should auld acquaintance be forgot.

A bride's first thoughts:
Aisle
Alter
Hymn
(I'll alter him)
1950s

Puns

Generally speaking –
Women are generally speaking
1950s

A joke – Two women were sitting silently.
1950s

A Farmer's Notice in his Orchard:
Heaven helps those that help themselves,
But heaven help those that I catch helping themselves.
1900s

There were three gnus, mother gnu
Father gnu and baby gnu,
Mother gnu was shot,
Father gnu was shot,
Baby gnu was shot.
That's the end of the gnus.
Here's the weather forecast
1950s

> *This pun could well have it's origins in the popular song of the time 'I'm a Gnu' by Michael Flanders and Donald Swann.*

A Cluster of Berries

A tailor named Berry presented the bill before the usual time. The gentleman desired he should be shown in and thus addressed him; 'You have sent in your bill Berry, before it was due, Berry. Your father the elder, Berry, would not have been such a goose, Berry. You need not look so black, Berry. For you, (yew) Berry.
1907

Dubious Rhymes

He tried it on the sofa
He tried it on the chair
He tried it on the window-seat
But couldn't do it there

He tried it in the garden
He tried it on the path
There was nowhere he could go to take
His girlfriend's photograph
1950s

I love you in blue
I love you in red
But I love you the best
When you're snug in my bed.
1960s

I love you sincerely, I love you almighty
I wish my pyjamas were next to your nightie
Don't get excited and don't be misled
I mean on the clothes line and not in the bed.
1950s

I wish I was your teddy bear
Tucked up in your bed
And I was bare
And you were bare
And teddy blushed all red.
1960s

I wish I were a pair of stays
Around a winsome fairy

A Cluster of Berries.

A tailor named Berry presented his
bill before the usual time; the gen-
tleman desired he should be shown
in & thus addressed him:
"You have sent in your bill, Berry,
Before it was due, Berry.
Your father, the elder, Berry,
Would not have been such a goose, Berry;
You need not look so black, Berry,
  For I don't care a straw, Berry,
    For you, Berry."

Carrie M. Harris.
  Sept 15th 1907.

I'd pull its blooming laces tight
And squeeze her little Mary
1960s

John has a thing long
Mary has a thing hairy

118

John puts his thing long
Into Mary's thing hairy
1940s
Answer; John has a broom handle and Mary has the brush

Once a knight
Always a knight
But twice a night's
Enough
1940s

Two little pillows edged with lace
Two little people face to face
And everything
In its proper place
1940s

When at home and in the tub
Think of me and have a rub.
1960s

Many rhymes found in older autograph books are not suitable to recount nowadays because they contain racist remarks and use words which would be deemed offensive. Regrettably, especially before the Second World War, there was an assumption amongst many that British people were superior and people from other races were referred to using dismissive colloquialisms. Today most of these words and sentiments are unthinkable but at the time they were accepted without question. The rhyme below, though still non-pc, is one of the milder examples:

Many albums have I seen
Some are black and some are green,
But in India where I've been,
'All bums' are black.
1930s

Fun bag sold for charity during 2010 World Cup. It bears facsimile autographs of the British team's 'WAGS'.

CHAPTER SIX

Unusual autographs, doodles and cartoons

AS WE'VE SEEN from previous chapters, in more leisurely times people spent longer over their autograph entries and thought little of painting a delicate watercolour, still life or flower painting, or penning a long piece of poetry or prose.

They also often produced cartoons or creative novelty pictures based on popular characters of the day. Some of the more detailed paintings must have taken hours to complete so presumably the artist borrowed the album to work on at home.

Cartoons

Many of the earlier cartoons were skilfully drawn like the one by my grandfather (who had a strong sense of humour) on the second page of his niece's autograph book. The cartoon showed two page boys in their buttoned uniforms, one lying on the ground and the other standing on top of him. It was captioned 'The First Page on the Second Page' and dated 1919.

Another illustration by him in a different autograph album shows a fish leaping from the sea with the caption 'Please drop me a line'. Cartoons were often based on, or copied from, illustrations of the time. Sometimes they were credited with the original artist's name, but more frequently were signed by the mimic and passed off as their own work. During the 1930s Walt Disney was particularly popular, and sketches of characters such as Mickey Mouse, Clarabelle Cow, Horace Horsecollar and Donald Duck often featured in autograph. Another favourite was

Mabel Lucie Attwell whose postcards featuring chubby-faced toddlers with amusing captions were all the rage. Copies of these children regularly appeared in autograph books (some were rather amateurish but others were excellently drawn). Louis Wain's cats were also frequently featured, as were the animal trio Pip, Squeak and Wilfred. There were many other drawings in autograph books which were obviously based on popular cartoons and paintings of the period, and it's interesting to try to source the original pictures on which they were based.

An amusing drawing seen in an autograph book dated 1909 depicted two rabbits – a young male and an older one. The younger rabbit is saying nervously, 'I, err, should like to marry your daughter, sir.' To which the testy reply is, 'Be a little more explicit young man. I have seventy-five daughters.' Another dated the previous year, depicts the back view of a large and burly footballer. The caption reads, 'This full-back, whose name is Mick, Has indeed a powerful kick. He is very heavy, as you see. So please don't ask him out to tea.'

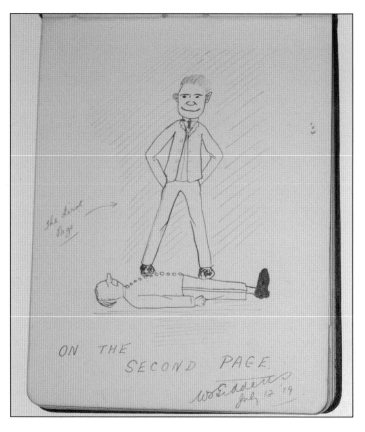

I ... should like to marry your daughter sir.

'Be a little more explicit, young man; I have seventy-five daughters.

Sincerely yes.

Wheeler.

Doodles

In the 1950s and 1960s, 'doodles' – sometimes known as 'droodles' – became a craze. These were ultra-simplified drawings of amusing subjects such as 'A giraffe passing a window' which just showed a spotty neck and resembled a snowstorm, or some circles connected with a straight line, which was a 'Mexican frying an egg'. The aim of the doodle was to make the sketch look like something else, hence the 'flower' which turned out to be 'four elephants sniffing at an orange' or the two lines and four semicircles which translated as 'a bear climbing a tree'. Some autograph albums of this period, especially those belonging to children, contain dozens of these doodles. In a way, the doodle cartoons were a throwback to the 1930s and before, when people had time to spare to draw a cartoon or work of art in an autograph album. Other doodles included 'Bear Hugging a Giraffe' (a spotted pole with four bigger blobs, which cleverly managed to combine the two classics – 'Giraffe Passing a Window' and 'Bear Climbing a Tree' into one picture). Then there was a domed head with oval eyes which turned out to be the back view of a lady scrubbing the floor, a round blob with ears (Rabbit Behind a Stone), a long rectangle with a small rectangle at each end (Washed and Ironed Accordion) and a rectangle with three blobs (Polar Bear Coming out of Lair). Dots were also popular and could be flies, fleas or bees.

Sometimes you come across earlier examples, such as some I recently found in a mid-1930s book. There was a drawing of an empty square (presumably meant to be a window) bearing the caption 'Above is an illustration of an aeroplane just out of sight', and a blank square, underneath which was written, 'This was a dog but he ran away.' One autograph book illustration dated 1928 showed a large round blob with various lumps and bumps with the words:

> What is this?
> A sack of potatoes?
> A sack of flour?
> No, it is our cook mopping the doorstep

Novelty pages

One clever submission to a 1919 autograph book is a coiled piece of blue thread labelled 'The Lost C(h)ord' underneath which is written 'Found by G M Dott 1919.' Variations of this often surface with the thread knotted or tied in a bow after being passed through two holes pierced in one of the book's pages. An autograph book from just after the First World War has

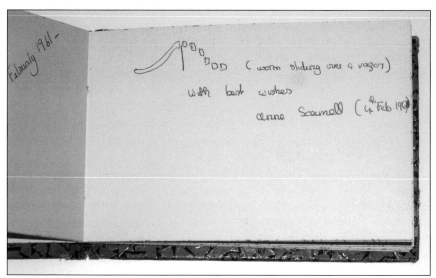

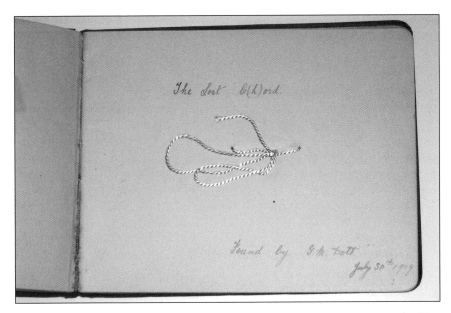

The lost c(h)ord.

Found by J. H. Lott
July 30th 1919

an ink spot in the centre of the page. At the top, a message reads, 'For Lovers Only', and below 'A Lonely Spot'. This was a quick and easy one to do, which would have invariably raised a chuckle.

Sometimes scraps, stickers and other items were used, though most people preferred to sketch or paint or write a message. Postage stamps were often utilised, with messages written beneath such as 'Stuck fast', 'Well stuck, by Gum'. 'I've stamped on your page' or 'Stuck on you'. One 1932 book had a matchstick stuck into it and the words, 'This is the most striking object in your book'. A similar sentiment was written in another album a couple of years earlier under a sketch of a grandfather clock. An autograph book dating from just after the First World War contained a 1919 entry that consisted of a lock of hair tied with silk. Underneath was written this rhyme:

> You asked for something original
> Something from out of my head
> And as I have nothing inside it
> Have a thing from outside it instead.

In 1919 a young girl created an attractive entry by pasting a silk Union Jack inside her sister's autograph book. Sometimes you come across pieces of embroidery or small tapestry squares; feathers, petals, ferns, leaves, sequins, tinsel, scraps of fabric, felt, pressed flowers, curls of hair,

Brittania rules the waves

your loving sister
Gladys
13.8.1919

dried grasses and even buttons. All kinds of things found their way into autograph books. Often they were used as part of a collage design, but at other times they would be incorporated into a sketch (such as feathers forming a crest on a bird or sequins as fishes' scales) or maybe they would be a 'memory jogger' such as a few dried flowers gathered on a picnic, or a lock of a friend's hair.

More frequently found are photographs below which the donor has inscribed his or her name, the date, and usually a loving message. This is a particularly inspired way of signing an autograph book, as if the friends go their separate ways, the photo will bring their faces to mind, even years after they parted. The photograph idea is still sometimes found in end-of-term and yearbooks from universities, colleges and sixth forms. These yearbooks often have spaces for signatures, comments and items to treasure from friends and teaching staff, and trigger many memories over the years. (See this chapter)

Celebrities often give out signed photos of course, and these are commonly found in autograph books. (See Chapter 8). It isn't a particularly new phenomenon either as some, especially those of music hall stars or musicians date from the early 1900s or before. There was often an overlap between photo albums, autograph albums, birthday books, visitor's books and friendship books. They were all 'memory joggers' and often contained signatures as well as facts, comments and photographs.

Ingenuity knew no bounds. One 1930s autograph book had a needle pushed through a page with the caption. The eye that doesn't shed a tear', while another book dated 1934, has a page covered in tiny spots. Next to them are drawings of a couple of flies and a note saying 'A fly has been here'. One entry dated 1936, and obviously made by a frustrated knitter, is spread across two pages. The first page is headed 'Instructions for making an original jumper'. On the opposite page is written a heartfelt 'Don't'! A sketch of a cigarette, dated 1928, is captioned 'This is the only thing I can draw besides my wage.' People obviously spent a long while thinking up new and clever entries for their friends' autograph albums, and most of these entries are seen time and again, so the ideas quickly spread.

Often seen is a folded page corner, with a 'secret' message beneath. Typically, the corner is labelled 'For girls only'. Underneath, the cryptic message reads, 'Boys are nosy', or 'Aren't boys inquisitive?' One lady describing her great grandmother's album says, 'I love this little oddity. A corner of the page has been turned down and on the folded edge it says "For Gentlemen Only". Underneath it says "Ain't women inquisitive" under which, in another hand is written, "No they are not". I love that! I'm sure it was a woman who contested the idea that women are inquisitive. I think it might have been my great aunt, who was quite a feisty lady. I can

just imagine her writing it, lips pursed!' In 1910 a lady – no doubt another with pursed lips – wrote 'The love of money is the root of all evil'. Underneath a wit has added 'Give me a big root'! A gentleman in 1908 wrote 'Believe but half of what you hear and see. Then he qualified it by writing underneath 'Good; but say, friend – which half is it to be?'

My own great grandfather wrote the following in his daughter's autograph book in 1919. The verse was written in an exaggerated swirly hand and crossed over and over, so that at first glance the pace resembled a page of scribble. An aunt who inherited the book believed it to be a page of nonsense, but I was not so convinced. I was sure such an erudite man wouldn't have scrawled but would have taken the opportunity to come up with something witty. I am pleased to say I managed to decipher it when I inherited the book:

> With paternal pride
> I here subscribe
> My name graphicalito
> Within this book
> Friends also look
> May pen their name or photo
> *1919*

Another clever drawing which appeared quite frequently around the 1930s was that of several straight lines with the caption 'Just a few lines from me'. (This quite likely cropped up in earlier years too, but was also very popular in the 1950s and 1960s). In 1920 a lady drew a row of sharp tintacks sticking upwards and wrote underneath 'Blessed is he that sitteth

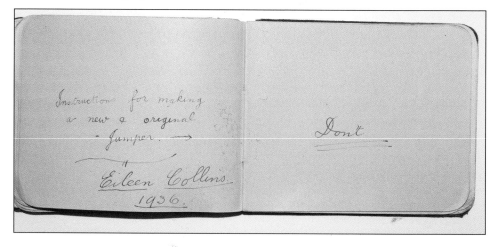

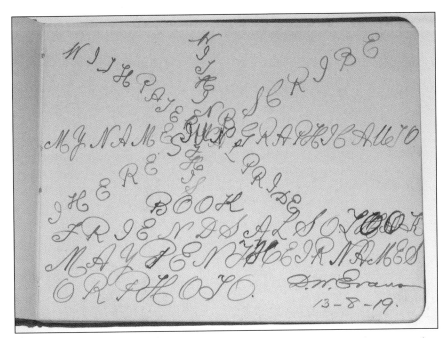

on these, for he shall surely rise'. One 1940s entry was a drawing of a ladder with the note 'I can't dance but will show you a few steps'. Even shorthand makes its appearance and sometimes you might find a message written by a secretary obviously proud of her newfound shorthand skill. If you're very lucky you might find a translation alongside it. Code also regularly turns up in autograph books. Certainly in the 1920s and 1930s, codes and clubs were very much in vogue, so coded autograph entries appeared, usually with the meaning written underneath.

A 'musical' entry seemed to crop up often in the early 1900s through to the 1940s. It consisted of three staves containing musical notations. These varied slightly, but frequently showed the symbols for flat, sharp and natural, with comments written alongside each stave.

They usually translated as:

Always be natural
Always be sharp
Never be flat
Or:
Sometimes sharp
Never flat
Always natural

In the days when many people were accomplished pianists, musical quips or even a few bars of music sometimes appeared in autograph books. For example, an entry from 1910 headed 'The Promise of Life' consisted of a few bars of music from this 1893 tune, together with the inscription, 'In remembrance of our impromptu concert'. The music for this song was written by Frederic H. Cowan, with words by Clifton Bingham. More simplistic is a drum drawn in a mid-1930s autograph album with the caption, 'Can you beat this?' or the drawing of a trumpet with the warning 'Never blow your own'.

Unusual entries

Sometimes rhymes and drawings are difficult to put into any particular category. Some autograph books have wartime entries, such as a drawing dated 1938 of a soldier hiding in a chimney pot, with just his head showing. As a bomb zaps towards him, he yells, 'Blimey, they've seen me.' One First World War entry dated 1917, is a skilful drawing of a regimental crest of the Royal Field Artillery, complete with the regimental motto, while a sketch dated 14 May 1914 seems to be a life belt garlanded with ivy with '1914' in the centre.

Other oddities include a clever drawing dating from 1936, of a mouse formed from a single line. The accompanying message is 'I'll do something to stop your grouse. Here's just a line which makes a mouse.' Another sketch, from the 1940s shows a shoe and the message, 'Always hold your tongue'.

Yearbooks

Yearbooks or 'class books' record school, college or university happenings throughout the year and include pictures of events and fellow pupils. There are designated pages for friends' signatures which are usually accompanied by an encouraging (or sometimes derogatory or even rude) message. Though sometimes seen in Britain, a yearbook is far more common in America where it is a more complex publication.

Trish Maunder, from Moorestown, New Jersey, says the American yearbook system is a very important part of the school year, and even elementary school years, 6-13, have them though it isn't till the children move up to larger schools that the books become larger, more complex

Selection of American yearbooks

and more meaningful for them. She said: 'The first two I have are middle school books called 'Making Our Own Path' from when my daughter Gabrielle was 13-14. The ones from High School are from age 15-18 and are called 'The Nutshell.' They are major production books, and have many photos, events and quotes. Each page is filled with collages, rows of photos or group shots. They show all the classes and faculty as well as student activities such as theatre, band, chorus, soccer, football or hockey. Then there are pages dedicated to lunchtime, field trips and candid shots. The list goes on. In the HS Yearbook there are also all the photos of graduating seniors.'

Trish further explained: 'Each school in each district will have their own name for their yearbook. 'Making Our Own Path' and 'The Nutshell' are just the Middle School and High School books for Moorestown Township. A yearbook is a beautifully-produced, high-quality, very heavy and expensive book. Parents submit photos of their children for various sections such as babies for the 'Guess Who' section, and other photos for the random photos pages. Otherwise there is a team of Year Book volunteers who run around taking photos of classes and activities all through the school year. It is a giant project. The books are bound and hard-backed tomes with glossy pages No one sticks anything of their own in them. The children only write their messages on the inside covers, front and back. They are regarded as 'sacred' in that way. There are hand-written notes by loads of friends at the front and back of all Gabby's books. The kids are passionate about each other and write wonderful things.'

End of term autographs from a British school 1990s

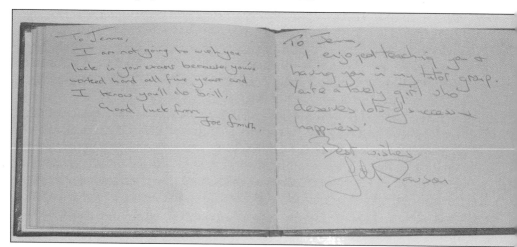

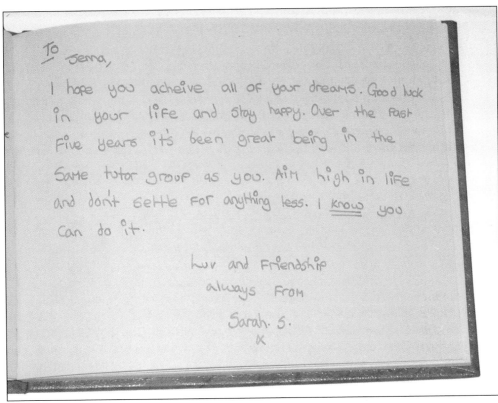

To Jenna,

I hope you acheive all of your dreams. Good luck in your life and stay happy. Over the past five years it's been great being in the same tutor group as you. Aim high in life and don't settle for anything less. I *know* you can do it.

Luv and Friendship
always from
Sarah. S.
x

End of term autograph from a British school 1990s

Amongst the messages in an American yearbook are 'Gabby, I am so glad we have stayed friends for so long. We have so many memories that I will never forget. Our friendship is priceless and I would not take back any of it for the world. You are an amazing person and I know you will succeed wherever life takes you! I love you and will miss you! Do it up at Wake! Karli,' or the more pithy, 'Gabby, Math was SO boring. Have an awesome summer. Brian.'

More commonly found in the UK is the standard autograph album, which once tended to be taken to school towards the end of the final term so that teachers and friends could sign it. However, this doesn't seem to happen so frequently now and is a loss of a tradition. When you do come across a British latter-day yearbook or autograph book, you will notice that the quotes are often much more flippant. But not always. There are some that are a credit to the schools and the pupils. Amongst the messages from my own daughter's Essex school-leavers year autograph book in the 1990s are such sentiments as 'Jenna, good luck in your exams and for the future. Have a great life and live life to the full. I am going to keep your signature so when you are a famous dancer, I will know you, luv Vicky,' and 'Jenna, I hope you achieve all of your dreams. Good luck in your life and stay happy. Over the past five years it's been great being in the same tutor group as you. Aim high in life and don't settle for anything less. I know you can do it. Luv and friendship always from Sarah.' I'm sure that my daughter will treasure her memory-filled book, just as much as those girls in earlier decades treasured their rhyme-filled albums.

Naturalist and presenter Chris Packham signs a book for Susan Brewer.

CHAPTER SEVEN

Collecting autographs of the famous – film and television stars, musicians and popular personalities

A LL KINDS OF signatures are collected nowadays, but here we look at superstars, pop stars and other media stars, and discover the best way of collecting their signatures.

Collection of signed photographs of media stars 1960s – 1990s

Autographs for all

Today, the cult of autographs is huge. Anyone in the public eye is likely to get an autograph book thrust at them – or maybe a scrap of paper, envelope, record, photo, receipt, crisp packet, arm, leg, breast, buttock or anything else that can be signed by the celebrity's pen. Many celebrities carry wads of ready-signed photos around with them to save unnecessary hassle but know full well that they could be destined for an internet auction. This means many celebrities will not now sign more than one or two autographs per fan. It must be galling to know that the so-called 'fan' isn't really interested in them at all but just wants to cash in on their autograph.

Autographs are big business and many dealers specialise in their sale. They usually concentrate on one or two fields, such as sport, celebrity or historical autographs. Sometimes celebrities will sell autographs at an agreed fee for charity. This is an excellent way of obtaining autographs, and also helps a good cause (though sometimes the prices can seem very high). Book signings are regularly held at bookstores and they are another good way of obtaining a signature which you know is genuine. It will cost you the price of the book of course, but at least you get a few moments with your celebrity and hopefully, a brief chat as well. Local newspapers and radio stations announce when celebrities are due to visit your town. Authors often visit schools or libraries and celebrities are regularly invited to fetes and shop openings. Charity events may have celebrities along to give the occasion a boost, though don't expect the autographs for free. It is only fair to make a donation to the cause.

Seeking the stars

So where do people obtain authentic autographs? The only sure method is by taking your book to the star and watching as he or she signs it. With a bit of luck, you'll also get a personal message at the same time. Nevertheless there are certain points to remember for even people in the public eye have a private life and although it might seem that they should always be on duty, even the most affable can have their off days. They might be tired, ill, have personal problems, be worrying about a sick relative, have recently suffered a bereavement or be undergoing a stressful period in their marriage or relationship. If you see a celebrity whose autograph you would like, then approach calmly. Don't run up excitedly so he thinks he is being mugged! Politely ask if he or she will sign for you. Have a pen and paper handy. If you meet with a refusal then say 'thank you', apologise for troubling them and leave. Accept there are some celebrities who, for various reasons, rarely sign autographs. By smiling, thanking them and walking away you will, at least, leave a favourable impression. Making a scene, swearing or throwing your autograph book at someone will make them even less likely to sign should you spot them again another day! But with luck they WILL sign, and maybe will ask your name and make small talk. If they do, then don't keep them chatting for too long. Thank them politely and leave. That way, it means that they will keep a pleasant memory of you. You may wish to follow up the rendezvous with a letter and thanking them for their time. Politeness works wonders and you might even receive a note in return.

If it is obvious that the celebrity is enjoying a private outing, perhaps with their partner or child, or dining in a restaurant, then think twice before you approach. Try to catch their eye and if you receive a smile, then you will probably be granted an autograph – but don't stay chatting and overstay your welcome. If you are blanked or glared at, then it just isn't worth antagonising them. And please, don't post your autograph book

Cliff Richard signed photos

Star Wars' Boba Fett (Jeremy Bulloch) signed photo

and pencil under the lavatory door, even if you know your absolute favourite star is within! Good manners would be to retreat from the cloakroom, hover outside the door and hope they are willing to sign when they emerge. If it is obvious that a celebrity is having an important talk with a business colleague or taking a phone call, don't approach until they are finished. You are far more likely to get a result from a polite request to a celebrity than you are by hassling them or by thrusting the book under their nose without a 'please'. If the star is 'on show' at a film premier, book signing or other public appearance, they will be more prepared to sign autographs as that is usually part of the deal.

Stage doors are the perfect haunt for autograph hunters, though often the major stars tend to be rushed in and out with bodyguard protection, especially if there is a large crowd of fans waiting. With lesser celebrities a word with the doorman will often get a message through, especially in smaller, provincial theatres. Sometimes you might be able to get a photo of the star, but do ask first as no one likes an unexpected flash going off in their face. Politeness and charm can work wonders on the most jaded of celebrities, but always bear in mind that there are some stars who are surly and unhelpful when away from the cameras. However, by far the majority appreciate their fans and are perfectly happy to sign a book and maybe have a quick chat.

If you are unable to visit a venue where your chosen personality is appearing, then you will have to acquire their autograph by other means. One way is simply to purchase a signed photo, record or other item from a dealer. The other way is to write to the celebrity. You will need to send a letter via their agent, fan club or, if they are a writer, through their publisher. If you are writing to a minor celebrity who may not receive many fan letters, then you will probably get a result from a standard polite

Susan Brewer (red dress) meets Pete Beale (Peter Dean) and Ian Beale (Adam Woodyatt) from EastEnders at a school fete, 1990s

letter asking for an autographed photograph, but if you are after a popular celebrity, then use some ingenuity. Make your letter stand out from the crowd. Use zany notepaper and envelopes in eye-catching colours, write about the celebrity in verse, comment on his career (and not just the basic 'I am a great fan and love your latest movie/book/record', but be a bit more creative). Do a bit of research. If your celebrity is a fan of Siamese cats for example, say how much you love them, too, and how you wished you could keep one but you live too near a main road. If he is into steam trains, then tell him about the trip you made on a preserved railway on holiday last year. Anything to break the monotony of the standard letters which he no doubt gets by the bucket load. Don't make your letter too long as almost certainly it won't all be read. If you stick to a page – handwritten if your writing is absolutely clear and legible, otherwise typed – the contents will be easily absorbed. Most important of all, don't forget to enclose a large – at least A5 size – stamped-addressed envelope with the correct postage to ensure the precious photo will reach you safely.

Drawbacks

The main drawback with this method is that as you won't be there when – or if – the celebrity writes the reply you can't be absolutely certain that the photo is personally signed. Busy stars might rope in agents, mums, girlfriends and fan club secretaries. Stars such as Elvis Presley often used machines which could auto sign several photos at once. In these computer-based times, it is quite possible to replicate a signature and make it authentic-looking. Often, though, you will be lucky. As I've already said, a friendly, chatty (but not too long) letter is more likely to get a personal reply than a formal approach, especially from older celebrities who grew up in the days before computers and emails and so are more used to answering correspondence by post. A lot of it is down to luck and catching the star at the right moment. Sometimes a small, thoughtful gift helps too. On several occasions I have received hand-written letters from celebrities which is a delightful and unexpected bonus. The knack is to make your letter a bit different and though a bright envelope might help, you will probably be even more successful by making an interesting or constructive comment about the star's career or hobbies. But don't forget the praise as most celebrities thrive on praise and adoration!

Often, in the heat of the moment, fans will approach a star for an autograph and ask them to sign their skin. Let's face it, male celebrities thoroughly enjoy signing the breasts, tummies and buttocks of an attractive young woman and it's amusing to have an arm or leg signed,

Autograph page signed by 1960s' pop star Mark Wynter

but is it wise? Although this is a fun thing which will provide a talking point for a few hours, many people have regretted this later. They have lost their chance of a permanent reminder. How distressing it must be to see the treasured signature dissolving into nothingness under the shower! You might be brave enough to have the signatures permanently tattooed, as a young British lady called Zoe Wade has done. Zoe gets her favourite celebrities to sign her body in thick black marker pen, then ensures the autographs will never wear off by heading along to a tattooist. She is quite choosy who she asks to sign her body and only the cream of the crop will do as she has no wish to be completely covered. Her arms and back now sport the signatures of such stars as Kylie Minogue, Celine Dion, Angelina Jolie, Ronnie Wood and Shirley Bassey, while a rainy twelve-hour wait netted Lionel Richie and U2's 'The Edge'. She was most thrilled with the Shirley Bassey autograph which was collected at a concert. Zoe was in the front row and reached up her arm so Shirley had to kneel down to sign –

Robbie Williams signed photo

an event witnessed by thousands. Although she gets the stars to sign in black marker, Zoe has the tattoos done in bright colours to reflect the stars' personalities or circumstances. For instance, Kylie Minogue's is in pink, for breast cancer. Her aim is to get the autographs of Madonna and Tina Turner and she is saving the tops of her arms for these, where they will easily be on show. Zoe seems to have accepted the hours of pain when the tattooist gets to work, looking upon it as a trial she has to bear if she wants permanent reminders of her favourite artistes.

It's really far better though to get a more conventional autograph on paper, a CD or book unless you want to look like an autograph book yourself! And what happens if you suddenly decide you hate one of the celebrities who have signed your body? You can hardly remove the offending signature to sell. If you are aiming to build up a collection of autographs, it's a sensible idea to invest in a small, high-quality notebook or autograph book with an attached pen kept constantly about your person. That way, you are always prepared if you happen to see your celebrity buying cornflakes in the supermarket or exercising their dog in the local park.

Inscriptions

Some stars will just scrawl their name in your book, while others will take time to write a personal message and maybe write your name as well, to make it really personal. There are even some who have developed their own special styles, which may incorporate a drawing or fancy insignia. Rolf Harris often produces a caricature of himself on a kangaroo's body, while wildlife presenter Chris Packham draws a crazy punk starling or some other creature. Comedian Johnny Vegas draws a face and the creator of the 'Peanuts' cartoons, Charles Schultz, used to draw a Snoopy. You might like to pencil in the date, and maybe the place, when you met your star, on the back of the page and, if the scrawl is practically indecipherable, it's a good idea to also write the star's name. It's surprising how difficult it can be to remember who signed what after a few years! I have a squiggle in my own autograph book which I regularly try to decipher. All I can remember is that it was written by a 'one-hit-wonder' singer, whose name must be in the archives somewhere, if only I could remember the song he sang.

A Buckingham cover signed by Roger Moore

Collectors often prefer not to have a personalised inscription, because, with an eye to the future, it's easier to sell an autographed item that doesn't bear the original recipient's name. However, many of us enjoy the personal approach and as we don't intend to sell, are only too pleased when we receive an autograph which is personal to us. If you are able to take a photo of the star at the same time, or maybe can get a programme or flyer of the event you have attended, it's a good idea to mount all the pieces, together with the ticket, under glass in a frame, to make a kind of collage. You can get a special non-glare glass, which makes it easier to see the items, and you can also buy special 'box-frames' which, as their name suggests, have a shallow box behind the frame, just deep enough to take a book or small memento like a key-ring or badge. That way, not only do you make rather a good conversation piece, it keeps all the separate pieces together.

Seeking autographs

Many years ago during a long stay in hospital, I began writing to favourite pop stars and authors for autographs and the majority replied with letters and photos. Decades before, in 1902, a young boy called Cyril Fellowes decided to relieve the monotony of his hospital bed by writing to the great names of the day, requesting an autograph. Cyril was thirteen years old and suffering from a broken hip. He was in hospital for three months and in that time wrote scores of letters to people such as author Rudyard Kipling, cricketer W G Grace and Robert Baden-Powell who was the founder of the Scout movement. Soon, the letters and signatures came pouring in.

Cyril was a middle-class lad in a Harley Street hospital and was fortunate to have a well-connected uncle who could get hold of the addresses. He was a polite boy and would apologise for his untidy handwriting, blaming his injury and the fact that he was lying in bed, and would end by asking for an autograph. His letters would read: 'I hope, sir, you will not think of me as a rude boy. Please excuse my bad writing, as I am in bed, having hurt my hip. I hope you will favour me with your autograph, if it is not too much to ask of you.' The response was amazing Lord Kitchener, at the time the commander-in-chief fighting the Boer War, explorer Captain Robert Scott, Australia's Prime Minister Robert Barton, author Henry Rider Haggard and anti-trade-slave campaigner William Wilberforce were just some of those who responded. Famous artist William Powell Frith sent advice with his autograph. He wrote something which autograph hunters should have engraved on their hearts: 'I have pleasure in sending you my autograph and a little advice with it. In applying for autographs a stamped envelope should always be sent for the reply. But this is not intended as a hint to you to send me one.' The various 'Get well soon' messages were housed in an autograph album.

Sadly, Cyril didn't have that long to enjoy his collection of famous autographs, because in 1913, now working on a rubber plantation in India, he caught blackwater fever, a virulent complication of malaria, and died at the age of twenty-five. His autograph album went up for auction and attracted a great deal of interest. It's worth trying to obtain autographs of modern writers, sportsman, politicians and artists, as well as media celebrities. One day, you might find that their signatures are worth far, far more than that of a current heartthrob.

Photograph signed by The Beatles

Who should I collect?

Some folk specialise – film stars, musicians, literary, politicians, royal, space, art, for instance – while others are happy to collect whoever comes along. Much of it inevitably comes down to money. How much are you willing to invest in your collection? It is perfectly possible to pursue this hobby on a shoestring. All you need is a notebook and pen and the patience to stand outside the stage door of a nearby theatre, or the price of a few stamps and some stationery. On the other hand, if money is no object, you might decide to invest £75,000 in a signed document by Ludwig Van Beethoven. It all depends on your interests and your financial status. Some people buy to invest, while others collect for pleasure, as a hobby.

Photograph signed by Michael Jackson

Michael Jackson signing autographs

As with other genres, in the media world it's the cult or 'megastars' who are most in demand. Autographs of people such as Marilyn Monroe, Elvis Presley, The Beatles (especially John Lennon), Bob Marley, Steve McQueen, Walt Disney, The Rolling Stones, James Dean, Bert Lahr, The Sex Pistols and Humphrey Bogart can all fetch thousands of pounds. As a rule of thumb, it's signed photos which are worth the most, as opposed to autographed album pages or signed documents. However, this isn't a strict rule by any means as many times a signed document will be worth more. It all depends and you would need to check with a reputable dealer, such as Fraser's of London. Also, although an autograph is worth a lot of money one year, it can quickly devalue if the star falls from grace. Sometimes a celebrity's records or films will flop, or maybe they will just go out of fashion. Many things can cause a star to fall from their pinnacle. A male star may feature in a court case regarding cruelty to his wife or have a string of affairs. He may even be imprisoned for some crime which reviles the public such as paedophilia, as has happened to a few personalities. The result was that they plummeted from favour, and their autographs lost any value they once had. So when you begin collecting, don't expect to make money from the hobby, certainly not immediately, anyway. As with all fields of collecting, autograph dealers need to learn the techniques and to study the market for many years. They need to not only predict traits; they must be able to distinguish fakes and forgeries.

In an auction held by Fraser's in 2010, the top ten bids showed the Beatles in first and third places, both with signed black and white fan club photographs. In second place was an official diplomatic letter in Japanese sent Hirohito, Emperor of Japan, to congratulate the newly-elected President of Panama. Fourth place was taken by a copy of a drawing of a vintage Gemini Capsule diagram signed by all three of the crew of the Apollo II mission; Neil Armstrong, Buzz Aldrin and Michael Collins, as well as fellow Astronaut Deke Slayton. Fifth was a signed cover of a 1969 issue of *Time* magazine featuring an iconic photo of Neil Armstrong as the first man on the moon. Pablo Picasso took sixth place, with a signed lithographic print and Princess Diana, seventh (A letter sent not long before she died, to a bodyguard who cared for her and her sons which was also signed by Prince William and Prince Harry). In eighth place was an important piece of football memorabilia; an album devoted to Sir Matt Busby's 'Busby Babes', with pictures and autographs. (Tragically, eight of the Busby Babes died in the Munich air disaster in 1958). Ninth was a signed postcard of Adolf Hitler and at tenth place was a signed photograph of Rudoph Valentino.

According to polls run by the American *Autograph Collectors Magazine*, some stars are much more likely to sign your autograph books than others. This might be well to keep in mind when you are standing in the rain or the bitter cold outside a theatre at a film premier. Amongst the most reliable signers are John Travolta, George Clooney, Jack Nicholson, Brad Pitt, Angelina Jolie, Megan Fox, all four Osbournes – Sharon, Ozzy, Kelly and Jack – Johnny Depp, Jay Leno, Rosario Dawson and Matt Damon. Interestingly, before his death, and contrary to popular opinion, Michael Jackson was a good signer when given the chance. According to the magazine, he always made an effort to interact with his fans and to sign whenever it was possible. Even in dangerous situations where he was engulfed by a mob, he would always try to stop and sign autographs.

However, there are many stars which, so the *Autograph Collectors Magazine* claims are reluctant to sign, refuse to sign, or will only sign at conventions when a fee is paid. These include William Shatner, Gwyneth Paltrow, Tom Hanks, Cameron Diaz, Nicole Kidman, Bruce Willis, Orlando Bloom, Demi Moore, Janet Jackson, Catherine Zeta Jones, Christine Aguilera and Britney Spears. Then again, you may catch them on a good day and find they are perfectly charming and willing to sign your autograph book. Everyone has their 'off days', though regrettably some people have more than others.

The popularity of various autographs rises and falls, just as the career of a star does. Some autographs will always, for various reasons, remain iconic and continually sought after, while others will burn brightly for a while before sinking to a more realistic level. Signed photographs of certain film stars such as the short-lived Jean Harlow and Marilyn Monroe, for instance, will probably always be in demand and sell for high prices, as will those of Stan Laurel, Oliver Hardy and Rudolph Valentino. Jimi Hendrix, Elvis Presley and John Lennon are pop music legends, and no doubt the premature death of Michael Jackson will ensure that the value of his autograph will rise.

In 2010, Fraser's auction house compiled an autograph 'Auction Top 100' based on total cumulative bids over seven postal auctions. At the top of the list were the autographs of the crew of the 'Enola Gay', the B-29 Superfortress bomber that dropped the first atomic bomb of the Second World War. It was used by the United States Army Air Forces in the attack on Hiroshima, Japan, in 1945. The bomb was code-named 'Little Boy'. The B-29 was given the name 'Enola Gay' after the mother of the pilot of the plane, Paul Tibbets. In second place was the ever-popular autograph of Neil Armstrong and in third place was Gemma Arteton, the British Actress who starred as the 'James Bond Girl' in 'Quantum of Solace'. This was the 22nd Bond film released in 2008.

It's interesting to see comedian Norman Wisdom with such a high placing (sixth). Patrick Swayze, at ninth place, is perhaps more understandable – he starred in the cult film 'Dirty Dancing', and his battle with cancer, resulting in his death in 2009, touched the hearts of thousands of people. Often, the death of a celebrity will result in a huge rise in the demand of his autograph and other memorabilia, and as a result, prices will also rise due to the inevitable dwindling of supply.

This list from Fraser's Autographs shows the Auction Top 100 listing, which has been based on total cumulative bids over seven postal auctions. The list was compiled in 2010.

- 1 Enola Gay - Tibbets, Van Kirk & Ferebee
- 2 Armstrong, Neil
- 4 Obama, Barack
- 5 Caine, Michael
- 6 Wisdom, Norman
- 7 Bacall, Lauren
- 8 Depp, Johnny
- 9 Swayze, Patrick
- 10 Bader, Douglas
- 11 Connery, Sean
- 12 Dean, Millvina – Titanic Survivor
- 13 Minogue, Kylie
- 14 Owen, Michael
- 15 Hooker, John Lee
- 16 Barrymore, John
- 17 Garland, Judy
- 18 Pacino, Al
- 19 William IV - King of the United Kingdom
- 20 Kelly, Gene
- 21 The Two Ronnies
- 22 Jolie, Angelina
- 23 Beckinsale, Kate
- 24 Bussell, Darcy
- 25 Burton, Richard
- 26 Jackson, Michael
- 27 Davis Jr, Sammy
- 28 Curtis, Tony
- 29 Cole, Joe
- 30 Cruise, Tom
- 31 Snowdon, Lisa
- 32 Page, Bettie
- 33 Craig, Daniel
- 34 Schiffer, Claudia
- 35 Christie, Agatha
- 36 Haley, Bill
- 37 Dench, Judi
- 38 Reeve, Christopher
- 39 Dempsey, Patrick
- 40 De Niro, Robert
- 41 Hartnell, William
- 42 Sampras, Pete
- 43 England 1966 World Cup Winners
- 44 Jordan
- 45 Lumley, Joanna
- 46 Watson, Emma
- 47 Dunst, Kirsten
- 48 Eastwood, Clint
- 49 Travolta, John & Newton John, Olivia
- 50 Duran, Roberto
- 51 Epstein, Brian
- 52 Valli, Frankie
- 53 Dunaway, Faye
- 54 Eaton, Shirley
- 55 Empress Eugenie De Monjito
- 56 Young, Alan
- 57 Pele
- 58 Borgnine, Ernest
- 59 Hoy, Chris
- 60 Jones, Chuck
- 61 Redford, Robert
- 62 Beckham, David
- 63 Hauer, Rutger
- 64 Lennon, John
- 65 Macfadyen, Matthew
- 66 Ferguson, Alex
- 67 Fishburne, Laurence

A Star Wars' Darth Vader (David Prowse) signed photograph

A Buckingham cover signed by Ralph Fiennes

151

Film Stars

If you decide to attend a premier or similar (as a ticketless fan!), be prepared. Take a folder with a clipboard, together with a few photos of the stars whose autographs you think you are most likely to obtain, or perhaps a couple of DVDs if applicable. You can download photos from the net and get them printed off (check for copyright first) or you can buy them from various shops which specialise in celebrity photographs. If you can secure a place at the front of the crowd at a major premier, then you just might manage to gather some top celebrity autographs. This is where to get the major stars of the moment; the Colin Firths, Hugh Grants, Tom Cruises, Keira Knightleys and Nicole Kidmans. One day the signatures of these stars could be very valuable indeed, but sadly as we can't see into the future it is difficult to forecast who will be the one to make our fortune. There are various things to take into account if you're going star-spotting at a major event. Firstly, and most importantly, get there early, not just half an hour before the event begins. You need to arrive several hours beforehand if you want to find a really good place and be in with a chance of being spotted by your star. Some people like to be as near to theatre doors as possible, while others prefer to be where the cars will stop, hoping that the star will be in a good mood as they emerge. This often works as the star will be 'fresh' and won't be exhausted from having already signed numerous autographs – though the plan can backfire if they have press interviews lined up. On the other hand, if you can get near the doors, you'll get good views (and photographs) of the celebrities walking up the red carpet.

You need to be at the front, or your star won't be able to reach your autograph book and you won't be able to get a good view or a photograph. Always carry a camera. If you have one of the small, slim-line modern digital cameras, you can keep it in your pocket or handbag so that it's instantly ready for use. Most mobile phones nowadays also have cameras, but the quality varies considerably. Even so, they are better than nothing. When you see your chosen celebrity approaching, it isn't a good idea to scream wildly and act like someone possessed. Keep calm but do say something. You don't want to be passed over, so smile and say 'Hello'. Or praise their appearance. With a bit of luck they'll take the hint and sign for you. A large banner, or something which attracts attention, can help, too. Dress smartly. Most of the celebrities will have put a lot of thought in to getting their wardrobe together for this auspicious occasion and they won't want to stand next to someone who looks unkempt and is wearing a scruffy T-shirt and paint-stained jeans.

Check the weather forecast. Although you will want to look your best if you are hoping to shake hands with a star who is going up the red carpet, if it's pouring with rain and you have been standing around for several hours, you won't enjoy the event if you're soaked and cold. Umbrellas are just a nuisance in a crowd and no celebrity is going to venture near someone who looks as though they are about to take his eye out with an umbrella spoke so take a lightweight mac, maybe a nylon one which you can fold up easily into your bag. Comfortable shoes are a must, too. High heels might look glamorous, but not only will they make your feet ache after several hours standing in one place, you might not be able to move quickly if you're tottering in stilettos if the crowd suddenly surges forward. Take a drink with you, preferably not alcohol as you don't want to blast your star with a gust of beery breath and also, it might not look good if you pass out in front of him on the red carpet! It's also good to have something to eat; not a picnic, something less messy. Even a tube of peppermints will stop hunger pangs. Finally, you need the two most important items – your autograph book and a pen. And if you don't get the autograph you're after, well, there is always another day.

The top film star autographs belong to the golden greats; those stars who illuminated the screen before they flickered and died. Right up there at the very top is Marilyn Monroe. Her autograph can fetch £20,000. Imagine

Signed photograph of George Clooney

paying that for a single signature! Yet there are people around who do, which is why there are so many other people around only too ready to pass off forgeries. According to an American authentication site (PSA/DNA Authentication Services in California), only twenty-four per cent of Marilyn Monroe and Elvis Presley signatures they examined were genuine.

Marilyn tops the list of most-coveted celebrity autographs of all but because so many of her autographed photographs (which were written in blue, purple or red ink) were actually signed by her secretarial staff, it is vital to only buy from a trusted and reliable source who can guarantee the authenticity of the signature. Other stars from the film industry whose autographs command high prices (though nowhere near as high as Marilyn's) include James Dean, Steve McQueen, Bert Lahr (who played the cowardly lion in *The Wizard of Oz*), Tom Cruise, Clint Eastwood, John Wayne, Walt Disney and Humphrey Bogart. Of these, autographs of James Dean and Bert Lahr can reach prices of around £10,000, while the signature of the enigmatic Walt Disney sells for around half this amount.

Marilyn Monroe was born Norma Jean Mortenson in 1926 in Los Angeles, and by the 1950s was one of the most popular film stars. Beautiful, with a flair for light musical comedy, she was adored, and amongst her films were 'Some Like It Hot', 'Gentlemen Prefer Blondes' and 'The Seven Year Itch' in which she posed over a grating in a white dress, a classic image which to this day is irrevocably linked with the star. After various high-profile marriages and affairs, Marilyn Monroe was finally found dead in her bed in 1962, having taken an overdose, probably accidental. She was just 36 years old .

Hundreds of other film star signatures are collectable too. Amongst the

154

stars whose autographs sell for well over £1,000 are Judy Garland, Charlie Chaplin, John Wayne, Rudolph Valentino, W.C. Fields, Lon Chaney, Groucho Marx, Grace Kelly, Judy Garland, Errol Flynn, Cary Grant, Clark Gable and Frank Sinatra (some of whom could also be included under musicians). One particularly coveted autograph is that of 1920s' screen heartthrob Rudolph Valentino. He was known as the 'Latin Lover', and died aged just 31, provoking mass hysteria amongst his fans. Rudolph Valentino hated the crowds which surrounded him whenever he went and consequently rarely signed autographs, so his actual signature is very scarce. As with many other film stars of the era, publicity secretaries usually answered written requests for autographs and signed photographs with a rubber stamp.

Stan Laurel and Oliver Hardy memorabilia is collected by many people and because they are such iconic stars, there are many fake autographs around. Incidentally, be aware that fake autographs of stars can crop up anywhere. They are not just the prerogative of the internet auctions. They can be found tucked in amongst the genuine items at respectable collectables' fairs. A few years ago there were reports of a Laurel and Hardy film-still card on sale at a fair, which was a clever fake though quickly spotted by keen collectors as there were so many things which gave the game away. They included such faults as the signatures being wrongly

Signed photograph of Clint Eastwood

Signed photograph of Tom Cruise

Signed photograph of Laurel and Hardy

placed one above the other, (invariably, Stan Laurel signed by 'his' side of the picture, Oliver Hardy by 'his' side). A ballpoint pen had been used on this 1943 picture, yet Oliver didn't get one till 1947 (he bought it at the Ideal Home Exhibition). Stan Laurel used a fountain pen. Finally, the clincher was that the card had been printed in 1970, long after both men had died. (See Appendix I).

> *Laurel and Hardy, alias Stan Laurel and Oliver Hardy, were a famous Hollywood comic double act, who made their first film 'Slipping Wives' in 1927. They made over a hundred films in all. Their humour was very visual with the contrast between Oliver's vast bulk and Stanley's thin frame providing much of the laughs. Although the pair met in America, Stan Laurel was actually British, born in 1890 in Ulverston, Lancs. He was a music hall comedian for a while and worked as an understudy to Charlie Chaplin in Fred Karno's comedy company. Oliver Hardy died of a stroke in 1957, and broken-hearted; Stan Laurel never worked again. He died in 1965.*

Autographed photographs of Laurel and Hardy sell for around £2,500 from companies such as Fraser's, and because of the British connection,

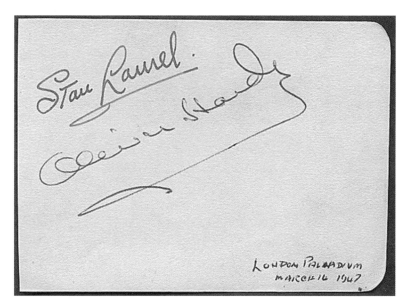

Laurel and Hardy autographed page

there is a great deal of interest in the stars in the UK. Although this information regarding fakes relates to Laurel and Hardy, much of it applies to any popular star. Once a name is known to sell for large sums, the forgers and fraudsters move in. The warning illustrates just how important it is for any collector to know the signatures of the stars he collects in detail and to be aware of little nuances and quirks which could point to a fake autograph. Familiarise yourself with the details and watch for tell-tale signs such as the positioning of a signature, the colour and type of the ink, and the type of photograph in use when 'your' star was active. That way, you can be confident that when you buy, you are getting the genuine article.

Buy from trusted sources. In 2006, auctioneers Vectis put up for sale a framed set of photos and autographs, relating to all of the actors who had played the part of James Bond to date. The actors included the first Bond, Sean Connery, the second, George Lazenby, the third, Roger Moore, the fourth, Timothy Dalton and the fifth, Pierce Brosnan. James Bond is a cult figure, and consequently the signatures of actors from the film are particularly collectable, especially the Bond actors themselves, and some of the Bond girls. Buying for a reputable auction house such as this, means that you can have confidence in the seller, and, should anything go wrong, you will have a guarantee which you can trust.

Musicians

The best – and cheapest – way to obtain these autographs is to visit the venue where you chosen star is performing. Nevertheless, as previously stated this is very hit and miss, as, certainly with a major celebrity, the security will be intense and it's unlikely you will get near enough to gain access to your chosen star. Certainly, in these days of heightened security awareness, many celebrities – even quite minor names – travel with a large entourage of bodyguards whose job is to prevent people gaining

access to 'their' star. You might, of course, be lucky and be able to obtain an autograph at a film premiere or similar event, but otherwise you will need to contact the celebrity's agent or management to obtain an autograph. Or, of course, you can buy one through a reputable source.

If you're happy to collect the signatures of lesser celebrities – and this term is something of an oxymoron, as many 'lesser celebrities' are still household names – then you may well be able to collect them by the traditional method of waiting patiently by the stage door. After all, this is the way that, years ago, people collected the autographs of The Beatles, The Rolling Stones and The Carpenters, which today

Signed photograph of Kylie Minogue

exchange hands for large sums. The trick is, of course, to try to spot celebrity trends with the aim of picking out those destined for a long career and not those who are ten-second wonders. Even so, it depends why you want to collect autographs. Most people like the thrill of speaking to their favourite personality and the visible proof that they have done so. The star has signed their book, or given them a photograph that they have personalised. This means much more to many people than collecting autographs of the famous just because they *are* famous. They collect because they like the celebrity, and enjoy the thrill of the chase.

> *The Beatles – John Lennon, Paul McCartney, George Harrison and Ringo Starr – began recording in the 1960s, and their raw, so-called 'Liverpool sound', the complete opposite to the bland solo artists of the time, quickly changed the face of popular music. The group soon reached a 'cult status', mobbed by thousands of fans wherever they went, but in 1970 they split up. Ten years later, John Lennon, the brash, outspoken Beatle, was murdered outside his New York apartment, and in 2001 George Harrison 'the quiet Beatle' died from cancer. Their autographs, especially John's, sell for thousands. Of the two surviving Beatles, Paul McCartney's autograph is particularly keenly sought after while Ringo Starr's is less so.*

In 2010 an auction house on the internet was offering a page from an autograph book that had been signed by The Beatles. John Lennon, George Harrison and Ringo Starr had signed in black ballpoint pen and Paul McCartney had signed in blue ballpoint. Ringo Starr had added 'The Beatles' above his name. The autographs were obtained at the ABC Cinema in Huddersfield in 1963 and came with an original press photograph of The Beatles backstage at the venue. The book also contained other autographs of pop stars of the era. Items such as this are very desirable and can command very high prices if the provenance is good. Another company was selling an early set of the Beatles signatures on a Parlophone publicity photograph. The postcard was signed on the reverse in blue ballpoint pen by all four Beatles and additionally

Autograph album page signed by The Beatles

Photograph signed by Elvis Presley

annotated by John Lennon, George Harrison and Ringo Starr with kiss motifs. This item was offered at £8,500.

Autographs of cult personalities will always be in demand. The reason they become so sought after can be because of several things. In some cases the signatures reach high sums because the star is deceased; prime examples include John Lennon, Elvis Presley, Marc Bolan, and in 2009, Michael Jackson. Another reason large sums are reached is because a group has split up and so the signatures of all the group members are worth more than single signatures. However, this isn't always the case. An album page autographed by The Beatles, for instance, might sell for £8,000, but a document signed by John Lennon could sell for a few thousand more. Elvis Presley is a cult figure whose popularity shows no sign of waning, even though it is well over thirty years since his death. Unfortunately, there are lots of faked Elvis autographs around and it is important for buyers to be on their guard and to always buy from a trusted source. Elvis was invariably surrounded by a large band of bodyguards and assorted hangers-on, and many of these have since admitted that they could fake his signature and did so on many occasions. This included the signing of autograph books, pictures and other items at his concerts or at the gates of Elvis's home, 'Graceland', while the star's secretaries have also confirmed that they regularly forged his signature in reply to letters requesting his signature.

In addition, apparently, Elvis's autograph is quite difficult to authenticate because there are so many different ways in which he signed. His signature varied quite a lot. With Elvis, as with other stars of the era, common sense is paramount. No one is going to part with a genuine Elvis Presley autograph for a paltry sum, so if you are offered one, it's odds on it's a fake. Also, remember the time period. Elvis wouldn't have used marker pens for his earlier photos as felt tips weren't on the market at the time. So he certainly wouldn't have signed in posh silver or gold. And a new, sparkling, glossy Elvis photo is unlikely to be genuine; colours weren't so bright and pure in those days, and there should, in any case, be signs of general wear. Always check with the seller. How did they come by the autograph? Did they actually watch Elvis sign it? When did he sign it? Be very, very wary.

Elvis Aaron Presley was born in 1935, in Mississippi, Alabama, USA, an only child as his twin brother died at birth. Later, the family moved to Memphis, and it was there that Elvis called in at a recording studio where, for four dollars, anyone could record a ten inch acetate disc. Studio owner Sam Phillips heard the music and later announced that he had found 'a white man with the Negro sound and the Negro feel'. Encouraged, Elvis was soon on the road to stardom, making records and plenty of 'sugar candy' type movies. Sadly, the singer became addicted to prescription drugs, and also became obese. He died in 1977, at the young age of 42. Today, his records still sell by the million as new generations discover his unique singing voice .

Other top selling autographs of stars in the music world include The Rolling Stones, The Who, The Sex Pistols, Led Zeppelin, Fleetwood Mac, Paul McCartney, George Harrison, Patsy Cline, Jimi Hendrix and Bob Marley. These signatures can fetch several thousands of pounds, depending on condition. Stars' autographs such as those of Eddie

Photograph signed by Rod Stewart

Cochrane, Marvin Gaye, Madonna, Freddie Mercury, Otis Redding, The Carpenters, Grateful Dead, Pink Floyd, Buddy Holly and T Rex are also highly sought after, and can reach well over a thousand pounds. Signatures of other big names in the music business – Cliff Richard, Tommy Steele, Rod Stewart, Elton John, Bruce Springsteen and Kylie Minogue – can reach the hundreds, while even the autographs of minor celebrities have a value. Everything depends on the photos or documents which they have signed, the circumstances of signing, the year of signing and last, but certainly by no means least, the certainty that the autograph is genuine. This is why so many stars are wary of those people who come armed with a dozen or so photos which they want signed, knowing only too well that most of them will end up on an internet auction. Frequently nowadays, celebrities will only sign a photo or similar if they can include the name of the intended recipient, believing it less likely that these are destined to be resold.

CHAPTER EIGHT

Collecting autographs of the famous – artists, classical musicians and writers

I T ISN'T JUST the signatures of today's media stars which people collect – there are many who seek out signed documents of 'stars' of an earlier age; classic writers, artists and musicians. And of course, their modern-day equivalents.

Artists

Collecting artists' signatures is rather an awkward thing to do, especially as they often have a painting attached to them! Many people collect signed prints, however, (See Chapter 11), or even originals. Invariably though, these are bought because of the attraction of the artwork in question, not because of the signature. But artists do sign other things, such as letters and postcards of their works, and this is a good area for art lovers to consider.

Particularly collectable are the signatures of 'classical' painters such as Paul Cezanne. A hand-written letter by him would cost in the region of £12,500, while a letter by Pierre Auguste Renoir or Henri de Toulouse-Lautrec might sell for half that amount. As with other collector's items everything is dependent on content and condition. Some artists are more 'in vogue' than others. Salvador Dali, Edvard Munch and Andy Warhol, for instance, are presently more popular than the Victorian artists Edwin

Letter hand-written by Claude Monet

Henry Landseer, John Everett Millais or William Holman Hunt. Sadly for William Turner, a document signed by him will only cost a fraction of one by Van Gogh.

> *French post-impressionist artist Paul Cezanne was born in Provence in 1839, and was a key figure in the development of twentieth-century art. Painting at the same time as Vincent Van Gogh, his work changed from impressionism to the use of larger blocks of colour, so morphing into a semi-abstract style, linking impressionism with modernism. He died in 1906 of pneumonia after being caught in storm.*

The signatures of Rex Whistler, Pablo Picasso, Claude Monet, Henri Matisse and John Constable – all household names and so eminently collectable – are sold for between £2,000 – £5,000, and sometimes more. Once again, it depends what they are attached to. In the case of Henri Matisse, for instance, a signed document might be around £3,000, whereas a signature alone would be £1,000 cheaper. However, as with all figures mentioned in this book, it is important to remember that the collecting world is very unpredictable, and things go in and out of fashion, so prices can go down as well as up.

Artist Andy Warhol's Campbell soup-tin art and distinctive non-representational colour silk screen portraits are instantly recognisable, even amongst those who are not art devotees. He was often asked to sign books of his work, photographic pages taken from a book and copies of his prints. These are becoming more and more collectable. Earlier than Andy Warhol, but just as idiosyncratic, is Edvard Munch. Munch's most famed work is *The Scream*, a disturbing picture of an open-mouthed figure clasping his hands round his ears in an attempt to drown out the swirling sea of noise around him. Finally, the flamboyant, twirly-moustached Salvador Dali painted striking, often bizarre images, featuring 'melting' clocks, angular branches and other intriguing images. The signatures of these three artists sell for around £2,000 depending on whether they are

Signed original artwork showing Captain Pugwash, by John Ryan

on postcards or paper. Obviously the price soars when on actual sketches or etchings.

> *Edvard Munch was born in Norway in 1863, and was a sickly child. He decided to follow a career in art, and quickly came to the notice of the press, who were very critical of his work. Munch experimented to find his own style, a form of Expressionism, and 'The Scream' is his most famous. Throughout his life he suffered mental problems, which are reflected in many of his works. Edvard Munch died in 1944.*

The work of the more modern illustrators and cartoonists often crops up on the market, as do their autographs. Some are more interesting than others; Charles Schulz, creator of the Peanuts comic strip, tended not to sign his full name. Instead he would write 'Schulz', which was how he signed his cartoons. He would accompany the autograph with a doodle of 'Snoopy' or other Peanuts character; a delightful, and very special memento for a fan. Rolf Harris (who could equally well fit into the 'music' category), also often draws caricatures with his autographs. The most usual depicts a kangaroo with the distinctive Rolf Harris head with spectacles and a bushy beard.

Autograph book signed by Rolf Harris, with his characteristic 'kangaroo' drawing.

Book signed by ballerina Beryl Grey together with a letter from her husband.

Classical Musicians

This is another vast collecting field. Some people concentrate on autographed album pages, photographs or letters, whilst other prefer to concentrate on collecting signed or original musical scores. Naturally, earlier musicians – Beethoven, Mozart and Bach, for example – were born well before the photographic age, but it is possible to find signed photos of such greats as Franz Liszt or Pyotr Tchaikovsky. Amongst the most collectable autographs in the classic music world are those of Elgar, Tchaikovsky, Sir Thomas Beecham and Sir Malcolm Sergeant.

Most auction houses and dealers in autographs publish catalogues, either on line or in book form. These are a delight to browse through because you never know what you might find. Classical music items could include such delights as a hand-written letter by Sir Edward Elgar to a music publisher informing them that he would be free to conduct works on a specified date and asking the company to enquire about fees, or there may possibly be an 1881 note from the Italian opera composer Giacomo Puccini. Composer of works such as *Tosca, Madame Butterfly* and *La Boheme,* he wrote (in Italian) that a few lines were missing from the sample of paper and that another stave – bells – needed to be added. Also seen in a catalogue was a hand-written letter from French composer Claude Debussy in which he was querying the payment of a bill. It just goes to show that even the greatest names in music suffered the everyday problems of ordinary people. It is the domestic items such as this that brings them to life. The same company was offering a beautifully-drawn musical quotation signed by French composer Camille Saint-Saens, known especially for *The Carnival of the Animals* and *Danse Macabre* and a signed photograph of the Italian Operatic composer Giuseppe Verdi, dated 1880.

A superb signed photograph of Pyotr Tchaikovsky in good condition and dated 1888 was up for sale for £15,000, while a hand-written letter from Sir Edward Elgar to music publishers Novello and Co. was a more affordable – though still beyond the reach of the average collector – £1,500. A Franz Liszt photograph, offered at £3,500 by a reputable dealer, showed the composer leaning on a table, his signature signed boldly across the base. A letter dated 1838 from Felix Mendelssohn-Bartholdi, about the sale of 'all my Copyright and Interest, present and future, vested and contingent or otherwise, of and in the 42nd Psalm set for Orchestra and four voices . . . whereas the said sum of fifteen pounds fifteen shillings hath been this day paid to me' was also offered, for just under £7,000. Items such as this are obviously important to collectors who specialise in musicians' autographs because it can be researched in depth, and relates to a particular piece of music. Therefore, it is much, much more than just another autograph – it's a piece of history to treasure.

> *Felix Mendelssohn-Bartholdi was born in Germany in 1809, started piano lessons at the age of six, first performed at the age of nine, and was soon a prolific composer. He wrote his first published work, a piano quartet, before the age of thirteen. At seventeen he wrote an overture to Shakespeare's 'A Midsummer-night's Dream', later returning to the theme when, in 1842 he composed the incidental music for the play, which included the much-loved 'Wedding March', still played at many weddings today. Mendelssohn died in 1847.*

Fraser's auction house handled the sale of a beautifully hand-written letter from Pyotr Ilyich Tchaikovsky to Ekaterina Ivanovna Laroche, the third wife of his close friend, the critic Herman Laroche. The letter was dated 19 January 1893, and begins: 'Dear Mistress Katou, Your letter was, as always, read with great pleasure and gratitude. I received it a week ago, upon my arrival in Brussels, and since then, partly out of laziness and

The flamboyant autograph of Piotr Ilyich Tchaikovsky

partly because of lack of time, I have not been able to express in a letter my gratitude for yours.' Tchaikovsky goes on to explain that he is going through some a kind of moral crisis, one from which he will either emerge victorious, or defeated, adding that his Brussels concert was a great success, but he became very bored, and travelled to Paris, hoping to remain incognito but had been overwhelmed, so is off to Odessa. He said: 'I have vowed to myself that I shall never go abroad again, except as a tourist, and absolutely with someone near and dear to me,' and signed off, 'I kiss your hands. Tchaikovsky.' This letter, accompanied by the original envelope and a translation, started at £18,500.

Richard Wagner featured in a mail order catalogue from one of the auction houses, who were selling a letter dated 1844. The letter, written in German and sent to a German publishing house, explains how the composer's opera, 'The Flying Dutchman', had recently been performed to enormous success, and that he now wanted the core to be published. Part of the letter reads: 'You've probably heard that I conducted the second performance of my opera on Tuesday in Berlin. As far as this opera of mine in concerned, namely The Flying Dutchman, I am resolved now not to delay its publication any longer for any reason, especially for artistic reasons. The performance in Berlin caused more than a sensation, it incited amazement. I want very much to be able to put my music before the public in black-and-white particularly after the remarkably successful Berlin performance. Also from the publisher's point of view, a more propitious moment than now will scarcely be found for publishing this opera. Let's conclude the matter quickly. It is especially important to me that this opera be placed before the public and not just sung and performed for it.' What a superb piece of music history, an honour to own, and something which could be purchased by any collector who had several thousand pounds to invest.

Also under this heading of Classical Music, we can include conductors, opera singers and ballet dancers. The autographs of Rudolf Nureyev, Margot Fonteyn, Anna Pavlova and Alicia Markova are sought by

D'Oyly Carte 1920s' memento folder containing autographed photographs

'balletomanes'. Amongst the conductors, Sir Malcolm Sargent is particularly collectable. He was very much adored by the 'Promenaders', and items such as signed photographs are popular. Another important collectable name is, of course, Sir Henry Wood, father of the 'Proms', while people such as Sir Thomas Beecham, Sir John Barbirolli and more modern conductors like Andre Previn, all have their devotees. Autographs of opera singers, especially those of the calibre of Maria Callas, Enrico Caruso, Feodor Ivanovich Chaliapin and Beniamino Gigi are popular, especially when signed across a photograph depicting them in one of their famous roles, as for example, a stunning picture of Maria Callas as Medea, selling for just under £900. The autographs of the three male singers, who are sometimes known as the 'Three Tenors' – Plácido Domingo and José Carreras from Spain and the Italian singer Luciano Pavarotti – don't sell for as much, and so are more affordable to collectors of this genre. It would be worth looking out for signed photographs of the three in performance, as items such as this should increase over the years.

Don't forget light opera too; fans of those prolific composers, William. S. Gilbert and Arthur Sullivan have plenty to look out for, such as signed

170

music scores, programmes and photos from the D'Oyly Carte Opera Society, as well as letters and notes from the composers. A delightful letter, sold a few years ago, had been sent by Arthur Sullivan to Lady Russell in 1892 and promised that the turkey and plum pudding will be ready when they visit, and apologised for his cook's 'mishap', which meant that he had to dine alone on Christmas day. He added: 'Hot formentations etc have restored my cook to good health and this morning she is desolée at yesterday's mishap. . . . Will you come tonight or tomorrow whichever is most convenient? And will Sir Charles come to play his besique beforehand?' The letter was written from a house where Arthur Sullivan was wintering on the Riviera, and presumably he had planned an English-style Christmas with his friends Sir Charles and Lady Russell, who were staying nearby. Due to his cook's illness, the celebrations had to be postponed. Other letters from Arthur Sullivan, which have recently passed through the auctions, include an invitation to a lady, Mrs Moore, which read: 'Your place will be reserved for you tomorrow evening, at my table d'hôte. 8 o'clock. I hope you will come.' The starting price was just over £500, while a much longer letter was sent to W. S. Gilbert in 1892, in which Sullivan reminds him of a suggestion made ten years earlier that they write a piece set in Egypt. He adds that he had witnessed a Dervish gathering, which, presumably would have been of use in *The Rose of Persia*. This is another important piece of musical history.

William S. Gilbert was born in 1836, and Arthur Sullivan in 1842, and between them (Gilbert was the lyricist, Sullivan the composer), they defined operetta in Victorian England. Their first major success was 'H.M.S. Pinafore', swiftly followed by 'The Pirates of Penzance', and their most popular work was The Mikado (1885) which poked fun at British bureaucracy, but was placed in a Japanese setting. Impresario Richard D'Oyly Carte produced many of the works, and built the Savoy Theatre to present them. He formed the D'Oyly Carte Opera Company, which continued to perform the operettas till 1982. William S. Gilbert died in 1911, and Arthur Sullivan in 1900.

The D'Oyly Carte company sometimes issued memento folders containing autographed photographs of their performers, and these are something else to look out for. The photos showed the performers dressed in costume, ready for their roles, and must have made a delightful souvenir for eager theatregoers of the day.

Richard Rodgers and Oscar Hammerstein were perhaps the most influential lyricist and librettist of the American theatre, writing many major musicals. Amongst them were *The Sound of Music, Oklahoma!, Show Boat, South Pacific* and *The King and I*. Autographed photographs featuring them are sometimes available, as are those of that other greats of the musicals; George Gershwin, Cole Porter, Ivor Novello, Noel Coward and, more recently Andrew Lloyd Webber. The field of classical and light music is vast, to suit all tastes. Finally, we mustn't forget those musicians who don't really come under the 'pop' music genre, but are more jazz-biased, such as Glen Miller, one of the best-selling recording artists from 1939 to 1942, and part of what we now refer to as 'Big Band' sound. Glenn Miller's final fate has never been resolved, but it is believed he crashed his plane into the English Channel in 1944. Signed photos of him are extremely collectable.

Literary

This is yet another vast category, ranging from classic names such as Rudyard Kipling, Charlotte Bronte, Jane Austen, Robert Louis Stevenson and Charles Dickens, through to modern authors. There is scope here. If you chance on an author who is not yet particularly famed, yet has potential – think J.K. Rowlings – you could be sitting on a nest egg! Modern authors often can be found at book signings, literary conferences or poetry readings, whilst, for the classic writers you will need to buy from a qualified dealer.

The rarest signature of all is that of William Shakespeare, as only six examples are known to exist. Three of those are on the same document – his will -which is housed at the National Archives at Kew. William Shakespeare's signature, assuming one ever came on the market, would set you back

Hand-written letter by Charles Dickens

several million pounds. How could you set a price on the signature of the

Skerryvore
Bournemouth.

Dear Madam,

This is a matter which I must leave to my publishers, Messrs Longman & Co, to whom I have forwarded your letter and to whom I beg to refer you for an answer. Will you let me add, in all gentleness, that your proposal to illustrate the verses seems to me excessive? But for this also, you will deal with Messrs Longman. I am heartily pleased you should have found the rhymes worth setting and I am

Yours truly
Robert Louis Stevenson.

Miss Carmichael.

Letter hand-written by Robert Louis Stevenson

Letter hand-written by Arthur Conan-Doyle

GRAND HÔTEL   Stockholm   19

TELEGRAMADRESS: GRAND
TELEFON: GRAND HÔTEL

Dear Sir

I read with interest your experience. Might I suggest that your colleague Mr Hannen Swaffer would prove an excellent guide in such matters. Then we might have your cooperation in convincing the world of this great extension of human knowledge which a small group of us never cease to urge upon the public.

Yours sincerely

A Conan Doyle

Oct. 30.

Buckingham cover signed by author Dick King Smith

most famed man in literary history, one, moreover, whose entire collection of hand-written documents amounts to – nothing? None of his personal papers, letters or manuscripts have survived, and the will is a standard legal document written by a lawyer.

> William Shakespeare's will was written in March 1616, and showed him to be quite wealthy. He left the bulk of his estate to his elder daughter, Susannah Hall, and £300 to his younger daughter, Judith. Much has been made of the fact that he left his 'second-best' bed to his wife Anne Hathaway, but this was probably the marital bed, the one he shared with her. The best bed would have been one reserved for visitors, maybe an heirloom, and it was usual in those days for the best things to go to the children. William Shakespeare died just a month after the will was written. According to legend, he had attended a 'merry party' thrown by his fellow writer Ben Jonson, and there had contracted some kind of fever (or alcohol poisoning). He was buried in Holy Trinity Church in Stratford-upon-Avon, and the stone covering the tomb is inscribed,
>
> > 'Good friend for Jesus sake forbeare
> > To digg the dust enclosed heare.
> > Bleste be Ye man Yt spares thes stones,
> > And curst be he Yt moves my bones.'
>
> Shakespeare's tomb is beneath the floor inside the chancel rail, but this favoured place wasn't due to his literary talent. It was because he was entitled to burial inside the church as he was a lay rector.

Photograph signed
by Rudyard Kipling

Buckingham cover signed by author Michael Bond

Other authors are easier to source. People such as Charles Dickens, for instance, or Charlotte Bronte, Beatrix Potter, Percy Blythe Shelly, J.R.R. Tolkien, Robert Louis Stevenson, Lord Byron or George Bernard Shaw. Naturally, it depends on where the signature is – on a scrap of paper or an envelope, for instance is going to cost a lot less, than, say, a hand-written letter from Charles Dickens discussing his latest idea for a story about a young lad rescued from the workhouse! Imagine the thrill, though, of having in your possession a few lines of poetry, signed by William Wordsworth, written at his Rydal Mount Home in 1846. This particular piece was recently offered by a leading London dealer for £3,250. You needn't even be an autograph collector to gain enormous pleasure from owing such an item; the sense of history, and the fact that the great man, responsible for so many celebrated poems, had actually spent a few minutes of his time inscribing this paper with a signature and verse, probably for a fan, is amazing. An internet auction site advertised an 1876 autograph letter signed 'C. L. Dodgson' to a Mrs. F. Morrell of Oxford, accepting an invitation to dinner but querying the date, and assuring her that 'It is wholly on your account – not for the sake of the pretty little niece. On the whole, I prefer plain children.' Charles Lutwidge Dodgson, alias Lewis Carroll, was the author of the children's classic novel, Alice in Wonderland.

One Charles Dickens item, which recently passed through the hands of Bonhams for £1,440, was an autograph letter written in the third person ('Mr. Charles Dickens'), asking Mr James Beale to have the goodness to send a receipt. This was sold together with three envelopes, all signed 'Charles Dickens', and addressed to Messrs Beale & Co, hosiers of Bond Street. All the items dated from the 1840s. A more controversial writer, Oscar Wilde, featured in an autograph letter, also sold by Bonhams, which had been sent to his publisher Leonard Smithers. The letter, which was addressed to 'My Dear Smithers', and signed 'Oscar', was responding to reviews of *The Ballad of Reading Gaol*. It read, 'I was very greatly pleased with Arthur Symons' article – it is admirably written – a most intellectual and artistic in its mode of approval, and method of appreciation – I don't think I shd. answer Henley – I think it wd. be quite vulgar – what does it matter: He is secretly jealous – He made his scrofula into 'vers libres', and is furious because I have made a sonnet out of 'skilly' – Besides, there are only two forms of writers in England, the unread, and the unreadable – Henley belongs to the former class.' It adds a thank you 'for the £4…. it was most kind of you to think of it. I have been rather unhappy and troubled, so have not written – but I hope to get all right this week.' The letter, which was sold complete with its original envelope, had been sent

176

from the Hôtel de Nice, postmarked 15 March 1896, and it sold for £12,000.

Sometimes unusual pieces can be found, such as a hand-written postcard from George Bernard Shaw dated 1941, which read: 'Dear Kate, If you can find a packet of P.R Breakfast Food, please send it to me. I have not enough left to last until Saturday. I hope you are enjoying another look at old Ayot. G Bernard Shaw'. Maybe you'd prefer a document written by the dashing Lord Byron in 1820 to some London bankers, containing instructions for the payment of the sum of £26 6s to William Fletcher, or perhaps an intriguing letter from poet Thomas Hood apologising for a late reply, due to 'a serious illness that indisposed me to all penmanship.'

Also from Fraser's was the following delightful hand-written letter from Rudyard Kipling to 'Timmins', which read: 'Elsie (Kipling's daughter), who is an incoherent animal at the best of times and, after her recent orgy in town more than usually incoherent, tells me that you've succeeded in selling the Brigadier (a cow owned by Kipling) not once but several times! The latest quotation she gave me was £35! I always said you had a magnificent business mind: and if this is true (the sale, I mean, not the mind) I shall bless you and anything over £25 which is my price you can give to any charity you like. You see – in case any one wants to know about him – the Brigadier is a nice-minded well set up child of Cow about nine months old... and his Pedigree is beyond reproach. He walks like the God Apis and his head is a treat to look at... The Bird had a Royal time with you and has told us some delightful things about it. I only wish she had brought you back with her instead of her new black hat...' Letters such as this, though not adding anything to the literary knowledge, can reveal delightful personal aspects. They seem to make a great man more human, and would be something very special to treasure.

You should be able to write direct to the modern authors; a note written to a favourite (including the obligatory stamped-address envelope) can reap dividends. Often, too, authors give readings at schools and libraries, so it's worth scanning your local paper to see who is visiting your town. You never know, that favourite of yours might one day become another J.K. Rowling. Children's authors are a good collectable; as well as the classics such as Beatrix Potter, A.A Milne and Lewis Carroll, there are many modern authors to choose from. Autographs of post-war writers, from the likes of Enid Blyton, Malcolm Saville, Anthony Buckeridge and Roald Dahl should still be relatively inexpensive. More recent writers should be easy to source – people such

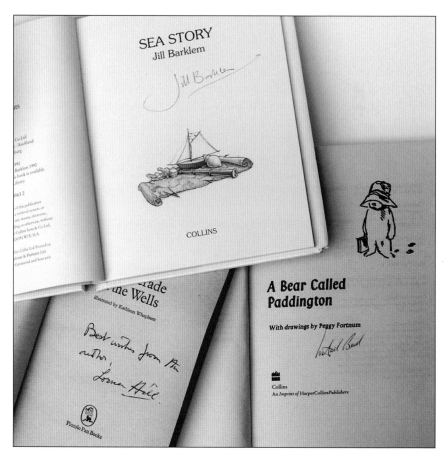

Collection of signed children's books

as Anne Fine, Jacqueline Wilson, Dick King Smith, Jean Ure and G. P. Taylor, for example. J.K. Rowling is the one which most collectors of children's author's autographs long for, but you would need to be very lucky indeed to find her signature, as it is already selling for a lot of money, especially on her books.

CHAPTER NINE

Collecting autographs of the famous –
military, political and royalty

T HIS IS A highly-specialised area. Many of the signatures collected in this category belong to prominent names from our past, names which are familiar to us from school history books or from television costume dramas.

Military

There are plenty to choose from in this category. Military could include commanders, admirals, and pilots – anyone connected with warfare. Often the letters and documents are signed by those great names which we learned about at school, names linked to battles and events which changed the course of world history. An album page, for instance, signed by George Armstrong Custer, a United States Army officer and cavalry

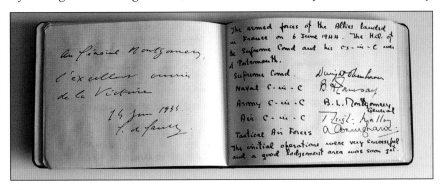

Facsimile of autograph book dated 1945 owned by General Montgomery with notes by Sir Winston Churchill.

179

commander in the American Civil War, was for sale not so long ago. Although Custer distinguished himself in the Civil War, he later led over 200 men into battle and the only living thing to survive was a horse called Comanche. For many years afterwards, Comanche appeared saddled but riderless in 7th Cavalry parades. This extremely rare autograph would cost around £4,000. Another rare piece, a document signed by British soldier Charles Gordon, written in Arabic in the 1800s, states: 'This sum is accepted and will be paid by the Treasury in Khartoum or Cairo, time, six months after today'. This is very desirable because notes by Gordon were usually burned, and it was a punishable offence to be in possession of one. It was very unusual for one to be smuggled from Africa, and this particular one bears Gordon's personal seal stamped in light green above his signature.

A collection of important papers dating from the Civil War sold for £20,400 through Bonhams in 2010. They included two documents signed by Oliver Cromwell – a letter ordering Hawkesworth to reduce the garrison at Warwick Castle by 'one Ensigne one sergeant one Corporall two Drummers gentll of Armes one gunners mate the Marshall & forty common soldiers' by the twentieth of the month, paying them in the meantime and securing their arms, and dated 8 October 1651; and a Commission signed by Cromwell as Lord Protector dared May 1655 and appointing Hawkesworth captain of a troop of horse of 100 volunteers. Other documents in the lot consisted of a letter signed by Prince Rupert, three documents signed by Sir Thomas Fairfax, a warrant signed by Charles I's judge John Bradshaw, and many other assorted documents, all of which were papers of Colonel Joseph Hawkesworth MP, and most addressed to him in his capacity of Governor of Warwick Castle.

The signature of Oliver Cromwell

An autograph journal kept by Allan Octavian Hume, Magistrate and Collector of the Etawah District, while on active military service during the Indian Mutiny, was estimated by Bonhams in 2010 at £15,000 - £20,000.

This narrative began in March 1858 and was a daily account of his defence of Etawah and his command under Colonel Riddell of a moveable column. The journal ended five months later when Hume, who was suffering from cholera, temporarily handed over the district to G.E. Lance. The journal consisted of approximately a hundred pages, and included a loosely-inserted lithographed map which showed troop dispositions. The map was printed with the caption 'Fought Feby 7th 1858/ Enemies Dead found and counted – 125/ Hung – 6/ One gun & whole baggage captured. (Signed) A.O. Hume. Feby 8th 1858'. Also from Bonhams was an autograph memorandum from Horatio Nelson dated 1803 signed 'Nelson & Bronte' which was intended for Captain the Hon C. Boyle of HM Ship *Seahorse*. It was headed 'Memo: for Capt: Boyle', and part of it read: '....to look into Toulon, and not necessary afterwards to get upon the exact rendezvous, the fleet from its present situation will probably not get so far to the Northward as the Rendezvous before it makes the Cape therefore I think if Capt Boyle gets the Cape side to bear NE for 8 Lg.s he will be sure of soonest Joining the fleet, unless another Gale should come from the Northward when if possible the fleet will get under Cape St Sebastians'. This enthralling piece sold for £4,320, while an autograph letter dating from 1801, signed 'Nelson & Bronte', and sent to Admiral Lutwidge sold for £5,760. This letter informed the Admiral that, 'the Assistance is also off Flushing so that our force there is very strong'.

Recently a signed photograph of a large group posed in front of a vast columned building with Lord Louis Mountbatten and his wife, Lady Edwina, seated in the centre of the group, dated 1948, came up for sale. Louis Mountbatten was the last Viceroy of the British Indian Empire and the first Governor-General of independent India. In 1979 he was brutally murdered by Irish terrorists who planted a bomb on his boat. One company was offering a hand-written note which read 'Thank you for your letter and the photograph of my Mother so well coloured by yourself. The war in Italy is going well and I hope that we shall be able to present its Capital to you as a somewhat late Xmas present. Good luck to you.' It was signed in the bold hand of B. L. Montgomery, General Eighth Army.

Political

Political autographs range from those of the great statesmen whose names echo through the years of history, to the latest, newest hopefuls fighting for a place in Parliament. This is where you need to use your judgement. Will that earnest young backbencher turn into the next Disraeli, Churchill or Heath, or will he forever be a virtually unknown failure, doomed to gather cobwebs? If your hunch holds good, then, who knows, you might have the autograph of someone who in years to come illuminates the history books, turning your scrap of paper into gold.

Which interesting autographs could you feasibly hope to obtain which are collectable? Those of the most historical importance will be the gems in your collection, though if you yearn for the signature of, say, Sir Winston Churchill on a photograph of the great man himself, be prepared to pay upwards of £5,000 for the privilege. A greetings card may well be less, or perhaps a short, hand-signed typed note. Not so long ago, auctioneers Fraser's were offering a typed letter dated 1946, from Sir Winston Churchill and addressed to the President of Columbia University: It read: *'I have received your telegram, asking my wife, daughter and myself to dine with you at your home on March 17 or 18. This would be a great pleasure to us, but I regret that I do not feel I can add to the engagements to which I am already committed during my forthcoming short stay in New York. In this I hope you will excuse me. Thank you so much for the kindness of your invitation, which it is most agreeable to receive.'* No doubt Churchill was snowed under with requests for his time, and it is to his credit that he could send such courteous replies of refusal. Sometimes, much more important documents or collections of letters turn up at auction, and these can sell for a premium; items such as these, written by such an iconic man who played an important part in the history of wartime Britain, are very sought after.

Sir Winston Churchill, born in 1874, is one of Britain's greatest twentieth-century heroes. He fought with the British Army in India and Sudan, and it was his journalistic dispatches from the Boer War that first brought him to public prominence. In 1900 he became a Member of Parliament, remaining an MP for over 64 years. However, it was during the Second World War when Winston Churchill really became loved by the British people. Serving as Prime Minister, his indomitable spirit and fiery speeches while leading Great Britain to victory, ensured he would be remembered as a renowned politician and a major player in our history. He died in 1965 and was given a state funeral.

Autographs from earlier politicians, such as Benjamin Disraeli, William Gladstone, Henry Palmerston, Robert Peel and Robert Walpole can sometimes be obtained from specialist dealers. Prices vary greatly, depending on the kind of document to which they are attached. Modern collectable politician's signatures include those of Margaret Thatcher, Harold Wilson, Ted Heath and Jeremy Thorpe, though none reach anything like the price of a Churchillian autograph.

Disraeli signature mounted together with a portrait

Perhaps the most desirable autograph from the field of politics is that of the first America President, George Washington, who took office in 1789. Many of the signatures of American presidents are particularly sought after, but that of George Washington is the 'holy grail'. An accounts document listing the payment of slave labour in the construction of a Canal at Shenandoah Falls was offered for sale and bore the signatures of George Washington, as President of the Potomack Company, and two fellow Directors. The document approved the payment of the labourers and listed their names, the sums due to each man and the total amount. This is where the fields of autograph collecting and social history meet,

Photograph signed by Winston Churchill

with an important and intriguing item documenting the pre-Presidential career of George Washington. This particular document was up for just under £30,000, though a straightforward autograph might cost a third of the price, if, of course, you can find one.

Another top-ranking American Presidential autograph is that of Abraham Lincoln. Elected in 1860, he is regarded by many Americans as one of the finest of the presidents. It was while he was in office that slavery was finally abolished. Documents signed by him, though not normally reaching the dizzy heights of those signed by George Washington, are still eminently collectable. A highly-desirable item was a partially-printed document signed by Abraham Lincoln as president, in 1864. This military promotion for Charles Meinhold as First Lieutenant in the Third Regiment of Cavalry was countersigned by Edwin Stanton as Secretary of War and bore a blue seal. It was priced at £15,000 a few years ago. Less than two weeks after this document was signed by the president, rebel troops raided Washington with the intention of capturing the Capital, but when they saw the massed Federal reinforcements, the Confederates soon retreated. Of the more recent US presidents, autographs of the charismatic John Kennedy, murdered in 1963, his wife, Jacqueline Kennedy, Bill Clinton, Dwight Eisenhower and actor-turned-president Ronald Reagan, all reach high prices. President Barack Obama apparently signed many pieces along his campaign trail, which are already changing hands for high prices. Presumably in years to come these will become high up on the political collector's wish list.

Abraham Lincoln, was born in Kentucky in 1809, and served as the 16th President of the United States from 1860 until his assassination five years later. He successfully led his country through the crisis of the American Civil War, preserving the union, and abolishing slavery. He held strong honest principles, and these, coupled with the shock of his murder when at the peak of his career, helped ensure that Abraham Lincoln's name went down in America's history as one of their greatest of statesmen.

Adolf Hitler's autograph on a photograph went on sale at Fraser's for around £5,000. Others selling for high prices included Leon Trotsky, Benito Mussolini, Mahatma Gandhi and Nelson Mandela. A typed letter signed 'A. Hitler' and dated 1931, which was sold through Bonhams in 2010 for £9,600. It was addressed to Sefton Delmer of the *Daily Express,* and written in German. Translated, it began that he hoped, 'out of this crisis a new readiness will grow up in Britain to submit the past twelve years to a reappraisal. I should be happy, if as a result of this the unhappy war, psychosis could be overcome on such a scale as to permit the realisation of the truly cordial relationship between the British and the German peoples so eagerly desired by myself and my movement.' He regretfully declines the invitation to contribute an article to the Daily Express, saying, 'Greatly as I am honoured by your kind invitation that I should express my views concerning the present crisis in Britain, my misgivings about undertaking the task are no less great. I am afraid part of the British public might consider it presumptuous of me, were I as a German to put forward views in a British newspaper which in conformity

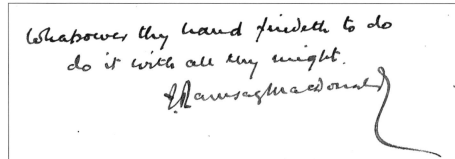

An autograph by Ramsay MacDonald

with my knowledge and my conscience can only be a criticism of political measures and proceedings, approved up to now by a large part of the British people.'

Fashions in political autographs, just as with celebrity autographs, rise and fall. If a famed or well-loved politician dies, demand for his autograph will rise for a while before it settles to a more sensible level. As with all autographs, it is vital to ensure their authenticity and to buy from a reputable seller. Many politicians send letters to their constituents, often in random mailings, and though the signatures may look correct, be aware that they are often replicated using a computer, or signed by a secretary.

Royalty

An autograph by Queen Elizabeth I is probably the most sought after of all royal autographs. Not only is it attractive and distinctive with its bevy of s-shaped curls and elaborate 'E', its creator must be the most dynamic woman is history. During her reign England rose to great power, although many believe that towards the end of her reign, when she became unpredictable and dangerous, Elizabeth was suffering from lead poisoning to the brain, caused by the white 'paint' she smeared over her face. Another particularly evocative royal is King Charles II. Amazingly, autographed documents from these larger-than-life people whose names dominate our history, can still be purchased from dealers, at a price. Some members of the Royal Family seem more iconic than others, regardless of the rarity of their autograph; these are the kings and queens who have a special aura. It's interesting to note that documents bearing the autograph of Queen Victoria are more sought-after and more valuable than those of her uncle William IV, even though there are far more of Queen Victoria's in existence.

Specialist dealers regularly have royal bits and pieces for sale from letters to signed photographs, and from greetings cards to documents. Sometimes the items are of historical interest, whereas other items are more personal, often letters of thanks or condolence. Amongst the more modern royal items is Princess Diana memorabilia. Anything signed with the name of this beautiful princess who died so young, seems touched with a special kind of magic and can command a high price. Her letters and Christmas cards signed in her characteristic clear round handwriting, often come up for sale, while photographs of her bearing her signature, are also very much in demand and consequently sell for thousands of pounds.

A superb offering from an auction company was an unusual manuscript document from Charles II, sent from Whitehall in 1682. In it, the King informs '. . . the Ranger of Keepers of Our Parkes Woodstocke' that 'Our Will and Pleasure is that you kill and deliver unto the Bearer one

Photograph signed by Queen Victoria

187

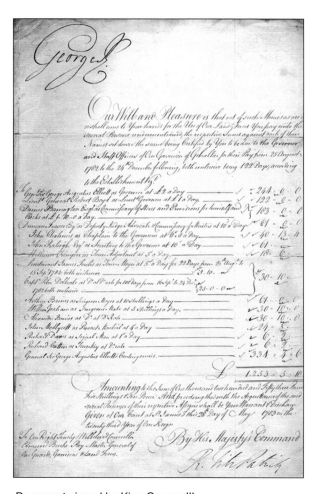

Document signed by King George III

fat Buck of this Season, and for so doing this shall be your Warrant.'
Clearly signed by Charles, the letter had been professionally mounted
together with an image of the King, and the starting price was £2,250. An
intimate letter from a later King, Edward VIII, who abdicated before his
coronation, was also on offer. Written in thick pencil to Mrs Freda Dudley
Ward, part of the letter read: 'My very own darling beloved one, somehow
your last letter, received at lunchtime yesterday, is the sweetest and most
divine of all, and how I love it and how hopelessly happy it has made me
sweetheart; I just don't know how to try to thank you for it tho. you know
I'm, trying!! . . . Your own E. only only can love TOI and he's so so entirely

thine how he worships!!' Edward refers to himself throughout simply as 'E.' and to Freda as 'TOI'. Freda Ward was the mistress of the Prince of Wales from up until 1923, remaining his close confidante until 1934 and the beginning of his relationship with Wallis Simpson. An attractive item was a posed photograph of King George V and Mary of Teck seated together with their young sons, later Edward VIII and George VI, on their laps. The card was signed by George V of the United Kingdom below his image and on his son Edward's behalf in black pen ink, and by Mary of Teck on her son Albert's behalf below their respective images and dated 1897 in Mary's writing.

Later royal offerings include two signed photographs, by Princes Anne and her brother Andrew, Duke of York, In her photograph, a young Princess Anne wears a puff-sleeved ball gown and she has dated the

Photograph of the Duke and Duchess of Windsor signed by Wallis

image 1994. It is presented in a gold frame and accompanied by a photograph of Prince Andrew, signed below the image, dated in his own hand '1990' and presented in an official green leather free-standing frame. Christmas cards from the royal family regularly come up for sale, such as one featuring a colour photograph of Prince Charles and Princess Diana standing either side of the young princes William and Harry who are on a pony. This particular card was signed by both Prince Charles and Princess Diana, and was offered at £1,500.

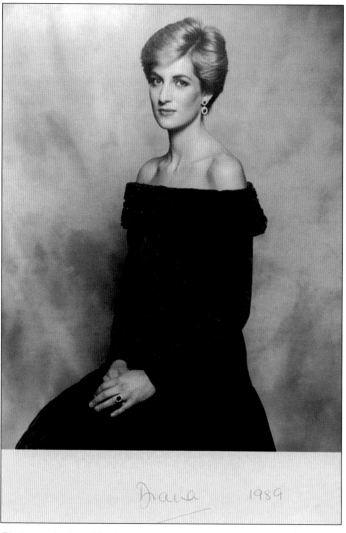

Photograph signed by Princess Diana

CHAPTER TEN

Collecting autographs of the scientists, sports stars and various other special people

ERE ARE THE people who have changed our world, blasting into space, building bridges and creating new means of transport. The sports section, a particularly popular category, remembers those past heroes of the cricket and football pitches, and the sportsmen of today. And under the 'Various' heading come those people, often great names in our history, who are not easy to categorise, but whose signatures are still treasured.

Scientists

The world of science embraces so many noble names whose discoveries have changed our life; engineers, chemists, physicists, botanists and a myriad of other people. Under this category come some of the most

Buckingham cover signed by Chief Concorde pilot Mike Bannister

sought-after of autographs in the hobby – those of the Apollo astronauts, especially the team of Apollo 11 who were the first to land on the moon. Probably the most popular science genre is that of space exploration. The prize autograph in that field is that of Neil Armstrong, the first man to walk on the moon, and forever remembered for his famous quote, made as he stepped onto the moon's surface for the first time on 20 July, 1969: 'That's one small step for (a) man, one giant leap for mankind.' Although he has probably signed his name thousands of times, he decided to stop signing autographs for the general public in 1994, and is a very private person who rarely gives interviews. So, demand outstrips supply, and his signature, especially when on an iconic photograph of him in his space suit, commands a high sum. Autographs of his colleague, Buzz Aldrin, who was second on the moon, are easier to source, but they too sell for a great deal.

Amongst the prize items offered from Fraser's was a colour composite print entitled *Pioneers to the Moon* which honoured the crew of Apollo 11. It was signed by Neil Armstrong, Michael Collins and Buzz Aldrin. A stunning collection of nine photos and one document, which bore the complete signatures of all twelve 'Moonwalkers', was also on offer. The autographed photos included Neil Armstrong, Buzz Aldrin, Alan Bean, Alan Shepard, Jim Irwin and Charlie Duke. Special pieces such as these cost thousands and thousands of pounds but would be the centrepiece of anyone's collection, as well as (hopefully) an important investment source. An exciting piece was a tiny, fragile section of Kapton foil, gold-coloured on the front and with a silver backing, which had been attached to the outside skin of the Columbia. The foil was designed to protect the astronauts from the extreme environment of deep space, and most of it burned off during the re-entry into the Earth's atmosphere. This tiny fragment was mounted in a presentation cover bearing the signature of Buzz Aldrin.

Other kinds of science-related items you might find for sale or auction include a short letter by Louis Pasteur (which was included with a souvenir requested by a woman in the 1880s), an autograph of Thomas Eddison mounted beneath a black and white image of the great physicist, or an album page bearing a signature of the Italian born engineer Nobel Prize winner Marchese Guglielmo Marconi, dated 1906. This latter was recently selling for £750.

Fraser's Autographs offered an interesting letter from Alexander Graham Bell, the Scottish-born scientist and inventor of the telephone. Part of the letter written in 1908 to a photographer for the Department of Agriculture in Washington read: 'Our understanding is that you will give me your services here as photographer for two or three weeks free of charge.. . . This was a generous proposition on your part.' He goes on to say: 'Mrs. Bell and I are looking forward with great pleasure to your visit here and we hope you will make our house your home while you remain. . . It would be better for you to supply yourself at my expense with everything required. I enclose cheque for One Hundred and Fifty Dollars – on account.' According to the sellers this invitation was probably related to the inventor's aeronautical experiments near his Nova Scotia home, which involved kite-like aircraft and resulted in the development of the hydrofoil. The same company were selling an important eight page Thomas Edison early Patent Document, signed and dated 1882. Thomas Edison was the inventor of the light bulb and many other scientific innovations, and at the time of the document installed the first large central power station on Pearl Street in New York City. The patent text was full of detailed scientific explanations as to how the invention works, and was signed with his full name, Thomas Alva Edison.

A significant letter written by Albert Einstein in his own hand and dated 1925, which seems linked with his theological position – and whether or not he believed in God, or in any form of god – was also available at the same time. Later, he was to say: 'I believe in Spinoza's God, who reveals Himself in the lawful harmony of the world, not in a God who concerns Himself with the fate and the doings of mankind'. This letter reads: 'While the materialistic aspect of the brochure is correct, its mentality is poor. The educated people were not big enough to repent their sins against the Holy Spirit publicly and officially; therefore one should not expect that from outside. In the more complete, cultural society deeply shameful situation, it is only fortunate that both parties were guilty of misdeeds. They should both reach out and shake hands, without either of them feeling superior over the other.' Einstein's signature sometimes is found on photographs and on various cards.

Of course, letters from the great scientists aren't always to do with their work, such as a collection of hand-written letters from famous English chemist and physicist Michael Faraday. These letters were addressed to 'My dear Caroline' and were signed, 'Very affectionately yours, M. Faraday'. It's interesting finding out about the private lives, as well as the public lives, of great personalities. It makes them appear more human, somehow, more like us. Often, you wish you could know the full story behind letters, such as this one offered by an American dealer. It was sent by Michael Faraday when he was in his seventies, to a Miss Crum. Part of the letter reads, 'Do not despise my small attempt to thank you; or correlate in any way the

Photograph signed by Buzz Aldrin

pocket book which I send you with the comfort you sent me. I rejoice simply in the opportunity it gives me of calling myself to your remembrance and if I were not afraid of making some mistake would use it more freely in respect of Mr & Mrs Crum your Sisters & others but my memory is you Still Yours Ever & truly.' Another interesting hand-written letter was sent by British physician William Jenner, asking a friend if he knew of someone able to stay with a young lady who needed help. Dated 1872, the letter read: 'Do you know of a youngish woman who accustomed to the charge of epileptics (not aware) could act & pass as maid to a young lady – the young lady once threw herself out of window. She is there for some time, been in Paris & proposes to continue there for sometime at any rate – Her friends are wealthy. The young lady will be living with friends. – If you do not know of such a person can you tell me where inquiries could be made.' William Jenner was the Physician to Queen Victoria and the Prince of Wales, and this letter is an example of some of the intriguing finds which turn up from time to time in autograph dealers' shops or internet sites. Browsing their

Mounted photographs signed by Apollo crews

catalogues is a fascinating pastime for anyone interested in how people lived in earlier decades, giving engaging insights to the social history and customs of the time.

Sports Stars

For decades people have collected autographs from their favourite teams or of their favourite sports persons. Often this is an interest that started in childhood, with autograph books thrust at players at the football match or maybe garnered from a school trip to Wimbledon to watch the tennis. Many of the autographs cost little, and are free if you visit the venue, though, as in any field of collecting, there are some top rankers. These are often the icons who have become household names - whether or not the household in question has even a glimmer of interest in the sport – but

Buckingham cover signed by Ryan Giggs

195

not always. It seems that some icons are more collectable than others; signed photos of Frank Bruno, for example, seem to go for little compared with some of the other well-known names. Footballers, especially, are much collected as football is Britain's national sport with a terrific fan base and some players' autographs are especially desirable. Signed photos from the likes of Bobby Moore, captain of the victorious 1966 England World Cup team, Pele and the Busby Babes are always in demand. More modern footballers such as David Beckham, Wayne Rooney, Ronaldo, Rio Ferdinand and Steven Gerrard are popular, too, especially when they are attached to an iconic photo or an item of memorabilia. (See Chapter 11)

Autographs of boxer Mohammed Ali, Wimbledon champion Bjorn Borg, racing driver Stirling Moss, cricketer W.G Grace, and golfer Tiger Woods are all very collectable. (It will be interesting to see if the 2010 scandal surrounding Tiger Woods affected his worth in the autograph world – if anything, it will no doubt make his signature even more

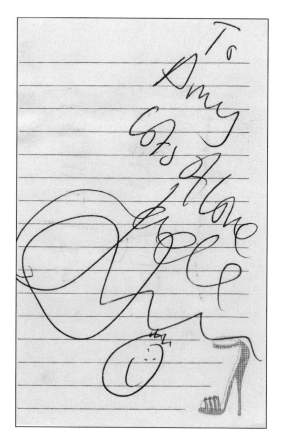

Jade Johnson's autograph

desirable!) There are many other top names from all fields of sport, and their signatures can run into hundreds of pounds, especially when they are on photographs. Amongst the signed photographs you might find for sale are a landscape colour photograph of Ronaldo, Zidane and Beckham, signed by Ronaldo and Beckham across their respective images in bold black pen ink, selling for around £300, a full-length picture of the legendary French footballer Zinedine Zidane (£150) and a superb colour photograph of Ronaldo pictured in the Brazil strip, signed across the lower portion of the image in bold black felt pen, selling for almost £250.

> *David Beckham was born in 1975, in Leytonstone, East London, and made his first professional appearance in 1992 at the age of 17, playing for Manchester United. During his time there, United won the Premier League title six times, the FA Cup twice and, in 1999, the UEFA Champions League. In 2003 he left to sign for Real Madrid, leaving in 2007 to sign with Los Angeles Galaxy. In 2008, he earned his hundredth cap for England, against France. Married to Victoria Beckham (nee Adams), who sang with the tremendously successful Spice Girls group, the couple have three children. Both David and Victoria are fashion icons and major personalities world wide.*

Items in the higher price range include a black and white photograph of the 1966 World Cup winning team that shows the players at the end of the match celebrating their victory. Bobby Moore is holding the Jules Rimet trophy as he is elevated on the shoulders of his team-mates. This photo was signed by Alan Ball, Roger Hunt, Gordon Banks, Martin Peters, Geoff Hurst, Ray Wilson and George Cohen. You might find a colour photograph of the England team signed by members of the squad, including Wayne Rooney, Paul Scholes, David Beckham, Ashley Cole, Michael Owen, Ledley King, Sol Campbell, Frank Lampard, Steven Gerrard, and Gary Neville, or perhaps a First Day Cover commemorating the 40th Anniversary of England's World Cup Victory signed by Pele.

Those 1950s' enthusiasts who were able to get the autographs of the Manchester United Busby Babes team squad, which was tragically almost obliterated in the 1958 Munich air disaster, may have earned up to £2,000. Items up for sale have included pages signed by eight Busby Babes including Roger Byrne, Mark Jones, Jeff Whitefoot, Dennis Viollet, John Doherty, Tommy Taylor, Ian Greaves and Ron Cope, and an album page signed by ten members, amongst them Jackie Blanchflower, David Pegg, Duncan Edwards, Dennis Viollet, and Bill Foulkes. Another item which was being sold featured a set of signatures across two small album pages

David Beckham signing autographs

and included such names as Matt Busby, Mark Jones, Eddie Colman, Duncan Edwards, Dennis Viollet, Bill Foulkes, Roger Byrne, and Tommy Taylor. The tragedy numbed Britain and the world of sport but sadly, it is events such as these that push up the prices of the victims' autographs, causing them to soar.

Other sporting items seen for sale include attractive signed colour photos of Tiger Woods taking a full golf swing on the green or posing with a golf club. an original 1964 European Grand Prix poster signed by many names (amongst them Graham Hill, Jack Brabham, Colin Chapman, Peter Rewson, and John Surtees) and a signed black and white promotional photograph of racing driver James Hunt. Photographs of sportsmen abound; you find autographed pictures of people such as Frank Bruno, Lester Pigott, Martina Navratilova, Greg Rusedski, Jonny Wilkinson, Anna Kournikova, George Best, Mike Tyson, Graham Gooch, Ayrton Senna, Alan Shearer and Michael Jordan priced from a few pounds to a few hundred pounds, depending on the person and on the photograph.

> *William Gilbert (W.G.) Grace was born in 1848 in Downend near Bristol, and has been widely acknowledged as the greatest cricketer of all time, credited with being vitally important to the development of the sport. He played for an amazing 44 seasons, from 1865 to 1908, during which he captained England, Gloucester Cricket Club, the Gentleman MCC and the United South of England Eleven, amongst others. He excelled at batting, bowling and fielding but it was in batting where he was to make his name, and he is considered to have invented modern batting. W.G. Grace was a medical practitioner and amateur cricketer, though he made more money through his cricketing activities than he did through his profession. He was one of the most famous celebrities of Victorian England, and he died in 1915.*

Amongst the top of the crop are the autographs of W. G. Grace, Malcolm Campbell, Donald Campbell, Venus Williams, Ayrton Senna, Rocky Marciano and George 'Babe' Ruth. Look out for signed first day covers, too (See Chapter 11).

One cover depicts a stamp showing the famous image of Bobby Moore being held aloft by his team mates after the victory over Germany in the World Cup Final 1966, plus images of both World cup trophies, and has been signed by Bobby Moore. It's also well worth looking through the ages of autograph books you come across – you might find signatures of football teams or top tennis players, or more quirky items such as a 1920s book containing the signatures of the Cambridge University Boat Crew.

Buckingham cover signed by Robin Knox Johnson

Various

Some autographs don't seem to slot easily into any particular category, so here is a selection of the kind of thing you might hope to find for sale if you search under the 'various' grouping. These autographs were all found on the internet and in auction catalogues. Amongst them was a delightful hand-written letter in faded black ink, dating from 1888 and signed by that doyenne of the nursing world, Florence Nightingale. She is approving the correspondent taking up a better teaching position, commending her for her kindness and confidence, and encouraging her to 'mother' the children for which she cares. What a wonderful congratulatory present it would make for someone who has just passed their nursing exams! A dealer in America offered a letter written by Florence Nightingale in 1891 to a Mrs. Robertson, which said how sorry she was to hear of 'Mr. Robertson's Influenza' and that she trusts he is quite recovered, and that Mrs Robertson is 'pretty well'. She then sends her thanks for the hampers, saying that everything was most welcomed, apart from the cream as the weather was too hot. Florence explains that she is going away for a while to her old home at Embley Park, Hampshire, so it would be best not to send anything apart from 'grass and flowers', though Mrs Robertson could also send eggs, which could be distributed.

Less expensive, but still poignant, was a photograph, signed by Mother Teresa with the words: 'Love others as God loves you, God bless you, M Teresa'. The German theologian and medical missionary Albert Schweitzer was awarded the Nobel Peace Prize in 1952. He spent much of his life at the leprosy hospital in Lambarene, Gabon which he founded. One of his items on sale was a portrait photograph together with a signature in blue ink clipped from the bottom of a letter.

Autographs of explorers, with their aura of adventure and bravery, are popular – maybe a hand-written signed quote from Ernest Shackleton, the British polar explorer who accompanied Robert Falcon Scott in his attempt to reach the South Pole. Later, Ernest Shackleton led an expedition which resulted in the destruction of his vessel by ice and an 800 mile voyage to seek help. The quote was penned on a vintage album sheet, and dated. 1918. It read: 'Dawn lands for Youth to leap; Dim lands where Empires sleep, And all that dolphined deep Where the ships swing. (Anon) E.H. Shackleton.' A half-length, black and white photograph of Sir Edmund Hillary, the first man to successfully climb Mount Everest in 1953, showing the mountaineer smiling, wearing garlands around his neck, and holding a tin mug, was also on offer. Maybe you would prefer a Nepalese First Day Cover with a cachet honouring the twenty-fifth anniversary of the first

Everest ascent, signed by Norgay Tenzing, who reached the summit with Sir Edmund Hillary in 1953? This too, has been just one of the many items available, as was a hand-written manuscript by mountaineer John Hunt, written in 1959 and offered for sale at around four thousand pounds. John Hunt was leader of the successful 1953 British Expedition to Mount Everest, and in this manuscript, Everest – the Unsolved Problem for the *Daily Herald*, John Hunt gives an overview on attempts to date to climb Everest by the north face and of a Sino-Russian expedition being planned for 1960.

Samuel Pepys is difficult to categorise. Is he literary – after all, he wrote a famous diary – or should he come under a naval heading, or maybe political? One item up previously for sale was a letter he wrote in 1669 to Edward Gregory, Clerk of the Cheque at Catham, which was the principal naval dockyard, requiring him to afford entry to thirty 'Caulkers for calking his Mates shipps at Chatham to preserve them against wather this ensueing winter' as well as 'twelve Ocarn boys and a pitch heater for ye carrying on of that worke. . . takeing care that as fast as the workes will admitt of ye discharge of any of ye said Caulkers, Ocarn boys, or ye pitch heaters provideing money to discharge them.'

Bonhams sold an autograph letter in 2010 from Captain James King, author of the narrative in the final part of Captain Cook's Voyage. The letter was addressed to 'Sir', so speculation is that it was sent to a naval superior, possibly to Sir Joseph Banks who, with Lord Sandwich, supervised publication of the voyage and was responsible for selecting King for the task. The letter – after asking the addressee if he could find out where he is being posted – states in part: 'I do not ask this for any other view than in order to arrange some little matters in regard to the publication of our late voyage, and for which reason I am not so solicitous to be informed of the place where as the time when we should go, should the former be a secret'. He then thanks him for many favours bestowed. Dated 1782, the letter sold for £5,760.

Anthony Ashley Cooper, 7th Earl of Shaftesbury, who lived in the 1800s, was a factory reformer and philanthropist who resigned his seat to visit the slums of London and to discover more about the living conditions of the working classes. One seller was advertising a hand-written letter responding to an enquiry about a suitable charitable bequest, suggesting the work of the Ragged Schools Union. In the letter, Lord Shaftebury states: '. . . none can exceed in value & importance, the Ragged School Union . . . if consideration be had of the large numbers it aids, the misery & ignorance in which they are, and the great success that, by God's blessing, has attended its efforts. In few cases, will a sum of money be so productive of real & lasting good, as in this.' Letters from all

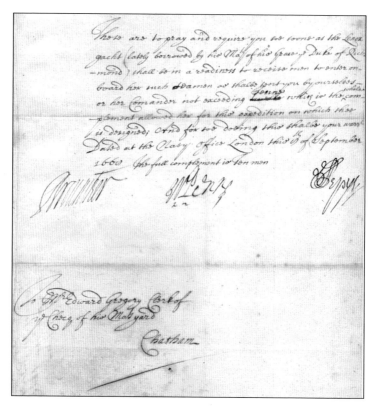

Letter signed by Samuel Pepys

kinds of people fall into the 'various' category, such as one from Octavia Hill, co-founder of the National Trust. She was an English feminist, pioneering campaigner for women's rights to university access, and a suffragette involved in the organisation of John Stuart Mill's 1866 petition to Parliament, which was the first to ask for women's suffrage. In a letter from an internet auction, she answered someone's question about the prospect their daughter going up to Girton College and explained the accommodation and the examination procedure. In 1869, she led the founding of Britain's first women's college, Girton College at Hitchin, Hertfordshire, which later moved to Cambridge.

Sometimes, signed photographs can be acquired of such people as Isambard Kingdom Brunel or John Logie Baird. Imagine looking at their signatures and knowing that the same hand which wrote the name, was also responsible for creating the Great Western Railway and designing some of our most classic bridges, or was the inventor of the world's first working television. One item with Brunel interest was a letter sent by Lord Spencer to Davies Gilbert PRS, in 1830, in which he asks whether 'Mr Brunel Jnr. the Son of the ingenious Mr Brunel the Engineer of the Thames Tunnel' could call on him, in order to show him his designs (for the Clifton Suspension Bridge). He states: 'The drawings . . . are very well worth seeing merely as beautiful drawings, but besides that they exhibit a specimen of young Brunel's Capacity as a Civil Engineer, which I have no doubt you will admit as doing him great Credit, & he is ambitious of being backed by so high an authority as yours as to the practicality and security of his Plan for effecting what really appears to be a stupendous Work of its kind, in the undertaking of which I understand that many of the principal & leading Men of Bristol & its Neighbourhood are greatly interested. If you should condescend to allow Mr Brunel to wait on you, he will be delighted at having that honour at any time or place you may appoint; & I think you cannot fail to be pleased with his Conversation or the subject of his Plans, as he is, though still young, a most intelligent and well informed Man'. A postscript reads 'Mr Brunel Jun.r's Residence is at No. 30 Bridge Street Blackfriar's'. Bonhams sold this letter for £3,120 in 2010. Brunel wrote references, too, such as a note dated 1841 which was

Note written and initialled by writer Thomas Hardy, addressed to Henry William Massingham, a journalist

203

sent to the manager of the Greenwich Railway containing a reference for 'The Bearer Thomas Houlian . . . employed at the Thames' Tunnel work from their commencement in 1825 to very lately when a reduction took place.' It assured the manager that 'The Bearer is a very industrious orderly and sober man who can be depended upon'.

Isambard Kingdom Brunel, born 9 April 1806, was a renowned engineer, especially famed for the building of the Great Western Railway in Britain. He also built many steamships, amongst them the first propeller-driven transatlantic steamship, and numerous important bridges and tunnels. His innovative designs were responsible for revolutionising modern transport, and one of his steamships, The Great Eastern, played an important role in laying the transatlantic telegraph cable in 1865. His father, Marc, also an engineer, employed his son to help with the Thames Tunnel which stretched under the River Thames. It was a dangerous project in which several men were killed or injured.

One of the most famous of Isambard Kingdom Brunel's projects was the beautiful Clifton Suspension Bridge, which spans the River Avon at Bristol. Other works of his include the Royal Albert Bridge over the River Tamar at Saltash, linking Devon with Cornwall, and Paddington Station in London. Brunel died in 1859 after a relatively short career, but one in which he left an enormous legacy still used and appreciated today.

Signed photographs of Thomas Edison, developer of the phonograph, cost in the region of four-and-a-half thousand pounds, while a signed photograph of Albert Einstein sells for double that, so these items are for serious collectors. Naturally, many people of historical interest died long before photography was invented, but some collectors and dealers carefully mount a modern photograph of a portrait of the person concerned, together with an autograph acquired from an album or similar. These can look extremely attractive and are a great way of adding appeal to what could be, in appearance, a basically uninteresting signature.

CHAPTER ELEVEN

Looking for and collecting signed items

ALTHOUGH WE TEND to think of autographs as signatures in small books with pastel pages, there are many other ways of collecting them. Signed memorabilia is big business nowadays.

Books

Collecting books signed by the author is particularly popular. As already stated, book shops often invite the author to sit at a table loaded with his books which they hope collectors and fans will come and buy. If he is lucky, there will be a long queue of eager buyers, all waiting for that precious signature, a word or two and maybe a photo as well. Of course, if the celebrity is not so well known, he might well endure several embarrassing hours while customers furtively eye him from behind the shelves, ensuring they don't catch his eye and feel obliged to buy. However, book signings can be surprising. In 2010, singer Leona Lewis was signing copies of her autobiography in a London branch of the Waterstone's bookshop chain, when she was attacked. Hundreds of fans had been queuing when a man came up and punched her heavily on the head in an unprovoked incident. She sustained bruising to the side of her head and was left shaken. The singer was unable to complete the rest of the signings. Thankfully, the majority of book signings are far less dramatic, providing a welcome opportunity for fans to meet their favourite writer or celebrity, and to obtain their autograph.

You don't always have to be at an event to obtain a signed copy of a book. Many times after a signing, you will find that a bookshop will have had extra copies inscribed which are stacked on a table bearing stickers

Book signing by actor David Prowse

'signed by the author'. Sometimes, they don't bother with the stickers and you will receive a pleasant surprise on removing a book from the shelves, something that has happened to me on a number of occasions. Once, years ago, I was in a department store in Epping, and I noticed some of the delightful Brambly Hedge series of children's books, by Jill Barklem, for sale. A notice informed me that her father was a manager at the store, and so was selling autographed copies. Another time I bought a few books from a car boot sale, and when I arrived home discovered one bore an inscription from comedian Kenneth Williams. When books are produced for a special event - maybe anniversary editions or a tie-in with an exhibition - inevitably a few signed copies are sold. Several years ago I found a commemorative Paddington Bear book signed by its author, Michael Bond. Biographies and autobiographies are especially worth looking out for. It's amazing how often you can find signed copies of these. So always keep a look out in your local bookstore or library for 'author signings' or events. That way not only will you soon build up an interesting collection of books signed by the authors but you will also have had the pleasure of meeting the writers.

If your favourite celebrity isn't due to visit your location then there are some booksellers who specialise in autographed books. You can get lists of these from the internet. They often feature signed biographies, such as those from Buzz Aldrin, Michael Caine, Vanessa Redgrave, Craig Revel Horwood or Ronnie Wood. Occasionally these sellers will stock rare and desirable tomes, too, maybe signed copies of classics including Lewis Carroll's *Alice in Wonderland*, Ian Fleming's *Casino Royale* and A.A. Milne's *Winnie the Pooh*. An important presentation copy of a well-loved classic was sold through Bonhams in 2010, for £32,400. This first edition of *The Wind in the Willows*, inscribed: *'To Foy Felicia Quiller Couch from her affectionate friend Kenneth Grahame, Oct. 1908'* was given to the daughter of the Cornish author Sir Arthur Quiller-Couch. Kenneth Grahame was a regular visitor to his house in Fowey, and it was whilst staying here that he was inspired to write *Wind in the Willows*. Interestingly, Sir Arthur Quiller-Couch is thought

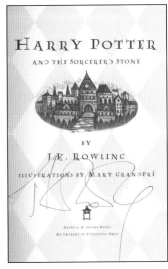

Book signed by J.K. Rowling

to have been the model for the character of Ratty for both he and Kenneth Grahame loved nothing more than 'messing about in boats.'

One of the most sought-after signatures amongst modern writers is that of J.K. Rowling, author of the phenomenally-successful Harry Potter series of books which recount the adventures of a boy wizard as he progresses through magic school. Books containing J.K. Rowling's signature can fetch thousands of pounds. It has been reported that she rarely signs books nowadays as she knows that if she starts she would just be signing non-stop. One very lucky man took his daughters to the book

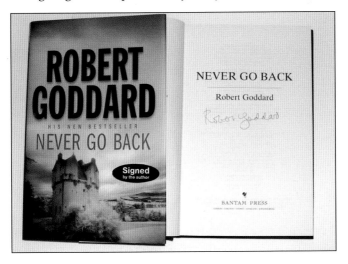

Book signed by author Robert Goddard

signing of another author, several years ago, when J.K. Rowling had just had her first Harry Potter book published. Hardly anyone knew the book, or who she was, so she was thrilled to be asked to sign. Consequently the book which she signed, an American first edition, bears a delightful message to the children as well as J.K. Rowling's signature. It is greatly treasured by the family concerned, but if it ever did come on the open market would no doubt fetch a tremendous sum. A major internet bookseller once offered a complete set of signed first editions of the Harry Potter books for well over £6,000.

Ceramics and other collectables

Collectables' fairs regularly feature displays of ceramics and other items, often in special editions or colourways made for the event. Frequently the designers or makers are on hand; ready to sign their pieces to make them even more desirable. If you are an admirer of a particular ceramic designer, then the acquisition of a signed piece is very special. Artists usually sign their original works – paintings and bronzes, for example – and although an artwork is normally bought for its appeal, a signature is nevertheless important, to verify the work. Some artists sell signed prints of their works. Devon illustrator and cartoonist Simon Drew who uses

Ceramics designer Peter Fagan signs a ceramic for Susan Brewer and daughter at a local store

208

pen and ink to depict animals with punning captions, sells autographed prints from his studio in Dartmouth. Collecting signed prints such as these from your favourite artists is a good way to acquire a collection if the originals are beyond your means. Though few of us can afford an original Van Gogh or Monet, there are still numerous original artworks to be found from a few pounds upwards – seek them out in galleries, exhibitions and showrooms. One day, that obscure signature on a favourite painting might be fetching sale room prices! Don't forget signed photographic works too. Naturalist and photographer Chris Packham sells signed limited editions of his photographs, so this is another collecting area; a photographic artwork with an autograph and dedication attached.

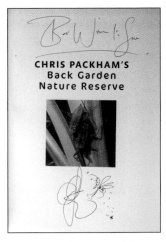

Book signed by naturalist Chris Packham, together with a drawing of a wasp!

Auction houses often have signed original cartoons for sale. These tend to come up frequently because a well-known cartoonist who is a regular contributor to several publications will have produced far more artworks than, say, a water colourist or oil painter. One of these was a white card featuring an original coloured drawing, in black ink and watercolour, of Bagpuss and Professor Yaffle. This delightful sketch was signed in black by Peter Firmin, and had been mounted, framed and glazed. Peter Firmin ran the Smallfilms studio, together with Oliver Postgate, from Firmin's eighteenth century farmhouse, and it was here that they produced several pioneering gems of stop-motion and drawn animation including *The Clangers, Ivor the Engine, Noggin the Nog, Pogle's Wood* and *Bagpuss*. Many favourites can be found in this way, and if you avoid the really popular classic characters – such as Rupert Bear – which

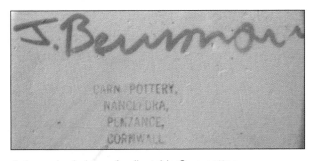

Autographed piece of collectable Carn pottery

209

Bagpuss painting
signed by Peter Firmin

have a huge fan base, and go for some of the lesser known, yet still familiar, artists, you may well be starting your own goldmine.

Signatures can sometimes be found on other items such as dolls and teddy bears, put there by the maker or the designer on limited edition specials. 'Designer dolls' are usually signed across the body by artists such as Hildegard Gunzel, Sieglinde Friske and many others. Teddy bears tend to be signed across the paw pads. Oliver Holmes, the owner of Merrythought, sometimes signs bears made by his factory for collectors, while Michael Bond, creator of Paddington Bear frequently signs the bears' 'luggage labels'. I have a signed doll that was given to me by Sarah Ferguson, representing the character 'Little Red' from her *Little Red* series of children's books.

Although these items would be desirable on their own merit and not just because they bore a name, the signatures are still an important and collectable adjunct. In some cases they can transform a 'common' item in to a 'rare' one as it is very desirable to have the signature of the artist, designer or creator of a work actually on the item in question. Ceramics

'Little Red' doll signed by Sarah Ferguson

artists such as Sally Tuffin, Lorna Bailey and many others often hand sign their work – though beware because some ceramic items frequently bear a stamped-on 'signature' as part of the imprint, and dealers may well refer to it as a 'signed piece', when all the pieces bear the same mark.

Clothing and sports items

A signed baseball cap or jacket that was once worn by a celebrity must be one of the most desirable of collectables because it is personal and a 'one-off'. But it's vital to get the piece authenticated in some way. Charity auctions, especially on the internet, have resulted in stars putting up all kinds of signed memorabilia, including clothing. Sometimes these items are sold by dealers who specialise in outfits worn by celebrities, or in costumes worn in films and on stage. One clothing specialist in America sold a top and skirt which actress Gwyneth Paltrow had autographed; absolute verification that the item was in some way connected to a star. Of course, you can't always be sure that the signed item you buy has actually been worn by your celebrity, but at least he or she will have handled it. Naturally, the majority of the items of 'celebrity clothing' won't bear signatures, as most people don't actually write their names across their outfits, so collecting celebrity clothing is beyond the scope of this book. However, sometimes you can find items used in films and which have been signed by the wearers to prove their authenticity. Fraser's offered a signed army helmet from the Oscar winning film *Forrest Gump* which was personally signed by actor Tom Hanks in black ink near the top of the helmet. Tom had worn the helmet while in combat as Forrest Gump in the Vietnam War. He gave such a convincing performance of the complicated character that he won an Oscar for Best Actor – adding to the other five Oscars acquired by the movie.

Things like T-shirts or tour jackets specially made for a series of concerts and autographed by the star, are desirable and sometimes auctioned. If you buy one of the garments on sale at the venue, and have a suitable marker pen, you might be lucky enough to get the star to sign it for you. In 2010, Fraser's offered a Las Vegas Hilton security shirt with a multi-coloured Hilton logo print. These special rare shirts were worn exclusively by the Wells Fargo Security Service members to distinguish them from Elvis' personal security members. The shirt has a gold badge attached to it number 76752, and was signed by Elvis Presley on the left breast pocket. What a prize for a devoted fan.

In the dance world, it's sometimes possible to obtain signed ballet shoes. Although these are usually sold to raise money for various causes –

Darcey Bussell auctioned some signed shoes for charity not so long ago – dancers often sign their regular practice shoes, just to ensure they don't get lost. Sometimes these make their way onto the market; you might be lucky and find an old pair marked with Nureyev's name, written in his own hand! A rare and desirable item for collectors of Princess Diana memorabilia was a bright yellow sweatshirt, commemorating Pope John Paul II's visit to London in 1982, and signed clearly across the front by the Princess. Another charity item, which was auctioned on Ebay was an umbrella which had been used as a prop in the popular television programme *Dancing On Ice*. The seller, who worked on the programme, was attempting to raise funds for the Macmillan Cancer Care charity, and had managed to get all the celebrities and skaters from the series to sign the umbrella. Amongst the signatures were those of Olympic skaters Jayne Torvill and Christopher Dean and the show's presenters Phillip Schofield and Holly Willoughby, as well as those of the high-profile judges. This silver umbrella was a special one of a kind collectable item for all *Dancing On Ice* fans.

Instructions for 'Elite' computer game, signed by co-creator David Braban

Sports clothing is another sought-after area, especially from cult sports such as motor racing. Apparently, race-worn items are particularly desirable, so if you could get Lewis Hamilton or Damon Hill to sign one of their old jackets or helmets, you would have a real treasure. Also collectable are signed footballs, cricket bats, tennis rackets and other sport items. Golf clubs signed by Tiger Woods, footballs signed by David Beckham or a cricket ball signed by Ian Botham are the kind of items collectors seek. Items signed by premium players can be very expensive, especially if the items were actually used in a match. Football and rugby shirts are often signed. In February 2010 a limited edition certified-England Centenary Rugby shirt, purchased at the England v Wales game on Saturday 6, February, 2010 at Twickenham, was sold via an internet auction. The shirt, which was unworn, was embellished with the original

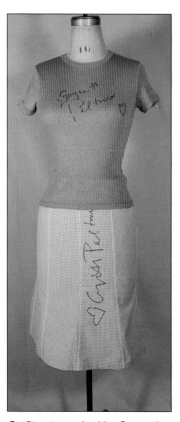

Outfit autographed by Gwyneth Paltrow

Jeans signed by 'The Swinging Blue Jeans' 1960s pop group. On show in The House on the Hill toy museum, Essex

autographs of the entire 32-man England squad for the game. It also was embroidered with a limited edition number and date, and came with a certificate of authentication with the corresponding numbers and dates. Thrown in for good measure was the match programme, promotional CD and the used ticket to the game. This complete lot was sold for £750, a very collectable autographed piece of memorabilia for someone, and typical of items which might come up for sale.

Other items seen include a white replica of the England football shirt which had been signed on the back in black felt pen by Steven Gerrard, and a superb cricket bat signed by twelve players from the current England cricket team. Amongst the signatures were M. Panesar, A. Flintoff, G. Swann, J. Anderson, R. Bopara, P. Collingwood, S. Broad, M. Prior, I. Bell, S. Harmison and A. Strauss. A friend was on a cruise a few years ago, and discovered that footballer Geoff Hurst was a fellow

Football shirt signed
by Geoff Hurst

passenger. She was able to get him to sign a replica 1966 England football shirt – what a marvellous item to possess, a lasting memento of that iconic football match. In America, some collectors concentrate on a really specialised field of collecting – baseballs signed by Presidents! One baseball was offered for sale which had been signed by President Bill Clinton in the July All-Star game, 1993. It was attracting high bids.

A leading auction house offered a white 2007 Formula 1 Australian Grand Prix television Pit Wall Access vest, signed across the front in bold black felt pen ink by Michael Schumacher, Fernando Alonso, Rubens Barrichello, David Coulthard, Kimi Räikkönen, Felipe Massa, Nick Heidfeld, Mark Webber and Jarno Trulli. The 2007 Australian Grand Prix was held at the Melbourne Grand Prix Circuit, Melbourne, Australia. Contested over 58 laps, the race was won by Kimi Räikkönen for the Ferrari team after starting from pole position, so this made a special collectable for someone. Also on offer was a 1997 dark blue official Ferrari baseball cap, signed in silver acrylic pen ink by Michael Schumacher and Jacques Villeneuve who vied for the title in 1997.

Ephemera

This word covers a multitude of items from football cards and postcards to posters and stickers. If you can arrange for your chosen celebrity to autograph a piece of appropriate ephemera, then that will make for an excellent collectable. Items which spring to mind are programmes for actors, tickets and flyers for pop stars, sheet music for musicians, picture cards, sports cards for sporting personalities and campaign flyers for politicians. I try to make a point of getting a programme signed when I visit the theatre, even if it entails a wait by a draughty stage door, because the signed items bring back so many memories. An amateur actress friend told me that the cast used to get each other's signatures on copies of the programme, together with a few comments, to make treasured mementoes. Often, ballet dancers and other performers do similar things. In years to come, those signed programmes are very special to

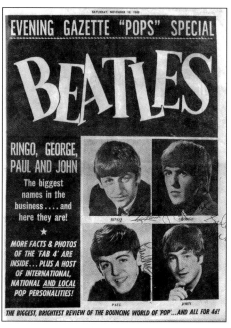

Copy of Evening Gazette signed by The Beatles

those who performed in the shows. People who are fans of one particular performer might compile a scrapbook of press cuttings, cards and other related items, and then ask the personality to sign it to make a unique memento.

I bought a bundle of 1900s' sheet music for a couple of pounds at a local antiques centre and was pleased to discover that some of the sheets had been signed by the composers. This is another collecting area. Devotees of musicians would ask them to sign copies of the sheet music after attending their concerts. Before the Second World War, sheet music was extremely popular – most people could play the piano, or were willing to sing as a 'party piece'. Many music sheets had attractive and colourful covers, and people would build up large collections. Nowadays, lots of collectors seek out the attractive copies, and if they are signed by the composer or the performer, then that's a bonus. (Often, though, they are signed by the owner, who might be an 'unknown', so a bit of research is needed – but usually these covers can be picked up really cheaply.)

Magazines and newspapers containing articles on the stars in question are also interesting to have signed. A copy of the *Middlesbrough Evening Gazette* dated Saturday, 16 November, 1963 and signed by all four of The

216

Beatles, was sold by Vectis for £3,200, while a copy of a magazine, autographed by Marilyn Monroe in 1960, reached an impressive £1,750 at an internet auction. If you know that a celebrity is visiting your vicinity, and you happen to have a magazine featuring him, it might well be a good idea to ask him if he would mind signing it. In years to come it could turn out to be of interest to collectors.

Sometimes, not just one item but a whole collection turns up. Often these comprise an eclectic group of items which link together to form a whole, and the most delightful are the unexpected 'off the wall' type collections, such as the 'Mr Turnip' grouping auctioned by Vectis. This included a mass of Mr Turnip BBC TV original hand-drawn Christmas cards and correspondence that have been reproduced in print, and used to send greetings to Mr Turnip's friends. There was a Laurey Puppet Theatre programme with patron Ralph Richardson's autograph and signed photograph, and a letter from Mr Turnip to an admirer, TV presenter, Miss Sylvia Peters, signed 'I remain your admiring vegetable, Mr Turnip'. Also included in the lot was a letter from Peter Hawkins, who was the voice of Mr Turnip, regarding the pilot episode of the Flowerpot Men, Peter Butterworth's autograph, and a Christmas card from Mary Norton, author of *The Borrowers*. This glorious mixture sold for £300 in 2007, and there were many other lots from the collection, all equally as enthralling.

Another quirky item owned by my daughter, is Sooty's autograph! This popular little bear puppet was performing magic tricks at an exhibition alongside his 'friend', Richard Cadell. One of the tricks involved a magic machine, which, with a tap of a magic wand, caused a photograph to pop out, specially signed by Sooty. Children love autographs such as this, and it's a way of easing them into the hobby. They will enjoy being given an autograph book and then collecting the 'signatures' of the various mascots which populate theme parks and other children's attractions.

Collection of signed 'Mr Turnip' memorabilia

Letters and cards written by Beryl Reid and Benny Hill

Instruments

Signed instruments, especially those used by famous musicians, are very special. To see and handle a guitar which was once owned and played by the legendary George Harrison, or one of the instruments belonging to Eric Clapton can be an emotional experience, especially if that piece also bears the legend's signature. Guitars seem to be particularly popular. I've seen a red Cruiser signed by Liam and Noel Gallagher from Oasis for sale, a Rolling Stones Talman guitar signed by all five Stones, an Acoustic signed by Hank Marvin and a Fender signed by Michael Jackson. Note though, that these pieces are often sold for charity or as collector's items, and might not have actually been played by the artist in question.

Guitar signed by The Merseybeats, on show in The House on the Hill toy museum, Essex.

Naturally, these instruments aren't cheap and can run into thousands of pounds. No doubt most are often purchased by ultra-enthusiastic fans of the artists. Others which have cropped up for sale include a gorgeous, red finish Epiphone Junior SG model electric guitar signed in blue felt tip on the body by all four original members of the Monkees: Mickey Dolenz, Davy Jones, Peter Tork and Mike Nesmith. James Taylor fans are also catered for. A natural wood-finish six-string acoustic guitar, signed in silver ink on the tortoiseshell pick guard and accompanied by a photo taken at the time of signing (excellent provenance) was selling at £1,250 not so long ago.

Letters

At the top end of the scale, you could pay a vast sum for an authentic letter from someone such as William Shakespeare or Elizabeth I, but, with a bit of luck, it's possible to get a hand-written letter from a celebrity for just the price of a stamp. Admittedly, in these days of computers, you are more likely to get a typed missive, but even so, hopefully the celebrity will have signed it. I began writing to celebrities a few decades ago, so am lucky to have received hand-written replies from the likes of Benny Hill, Beryl Reid and Kenneth Williams. Additionally, I have letters from children's authors, including Malcolm Saville, creator of the *Lone Pine* books, and Anthony Buckeridge, who wrote the *Jennings* sagas. It's always special to receive a hand-penned letter from a star. I have a brief note from Cliff Richard, chatty letters from actor Mark Wynter and a card from actor Paul Nicholas, all hand-written and all treasured.

Guitar autographed by Randy Crawford and Dionne Warwick, on show in The House on the Hill toy museum, Essex

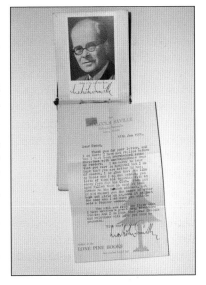

Letter written by children's author Malcolm Saville

219

Letters from current royalty tend to be signed by a lady-in-waiting, but are impressive with their royal crests. Unless you are privileged, you are unlikely to receive a hand-signed letter from Her Majesty the Queen or any of the higher-ranking Royals, though if you happen to be on a royal Christmas card list, then you might well be fortunate enough to receive a hand signed greeting, something to treasure. Quite often, MPs will personally sign their letters, even though a secretary will no doubt have typed them. Former Prime Minister Gordon Brown made news headlines when it was revealed that he took the trouble to produce hand-written personal letters to the grieving relatives of soldiers who had died fighting for their country. Historical letters are very special; imagine owning a letter which was penned by Charles Dickens, William Wordsworth or Jane Austin. Yet these items are available, for a price. It must be a wonderful feeling to know that a great author had penned your letter while he was writing one of his classic novels, or writing a much-loved poem. (See Chapters 7, 8, 9, 10).

Records

Records, especially those signed by the Beatles or Elvis Presley, can be very valuable, as long as the signatures are genuine. It's always worth taking along a copy of a singer or musician's compact disc if you are going to a performance, in the hope you can get it signed. As with autographs, it depends very much on the venue. It stands to reason that if you are attending a concert along with thousands of others at a prestigious venue, you won't have much hope of getting an autograph unless you happen to be friends with the security guard. If, however, a celebrity is giving a concert at a smaller venue, they might well have a record-signing session afterwards. A signature on a record can substantially increase the value of the item, especially if the signature belongs to a 'megastar', such as Michael Jackson, Paul McCartney or Elton John.

Celebrities often sell copies of their recordings to fans at the venue and sign them in their presence, so, for the price of a CD you can get a good collectable item. I once went to a jazz performance at a local theatre and was able to obtain the autographs of Humphrey Littleton and Helen Shapiro on CDs. In 2009, Vectis auctions sold a copy of a rare autographed 45 rpm single which contained the title theme from Gerry Anderson's *Joe 9* dating from 1968, with music by Barry Gray. It was in excellent condition within a black and white sleeve and autographed on the front paper cover. Amongst the signatures were those of Barry Gray, Wanda Webb (Puppeteer) and Shane Rimmer (Scott) and it sold for £90.

CDs signed by Helen Shapiro and Humphrey Littleton

Rare limited edition soundtrack from Babylon 5 signed by actress Mira Furlan and composer Christopher Franke

Rare vinyl single of title theme of Joe 90 signed by cast members and musician Barry Gray

Vehicles

In February 2005, a car was auctioned which had been won on a 'Children In Need' television programme. It was signed by many stars including racing driver David Coulthard; singers Elton John, Kylie Minogue, Shania Twain, Alison Moyet, Jamie Cullen, Donny Osmond, Lemar, Geri Halliwell and Katie Melua. Other celebrities who signed included groups Blue, West Life, Travis and Girls Aloud, actors Shane Ritchie, Amanda Holden and Maureen Lipman, television reporters Michael Buerk, Andrew Marr and Jenny Bond, as well as Ozzy and Sharon Osborne, Terry Wogan and Tony Blackburn. The car in question was a metallic blue, six-seater supermini, a three-month-old 2004 Honda FR-V 1.7 VTEC SE, and it later sold for £12,093.75. It had originally been the star prize on offer to those making donations to the 2004 BBC TV's Children in Need charity appeal, and was auctioned by specialist historic and collector's car auction house, HandH.

These autographed vehicle auctions are very popular in America, where in 2009 dozens of celebrities autographed a 'CSN Star Car' to help raise funds for the Child Safety Network, a charitable trust dedicated to

Honda car autographed by dozens of celebrities for 'Children in Need'

preventing child abuse, abduction and injury. Stars who signed the vehicle included Simon Cowell, Paula Abdul, Dustin Hoffman, John Cleese, Mickey Rourke, the Jonas Brothers and Rachael Wood. The CSN was celebrating its twentieth year as a national leader in the prevention of child abuse, and the campaign helped to generate awareness and to raise funds. An earlier autographed car, a Lamborghini, also raised a record $500,000 in 2006 for the CSN. The car was signed by such stars as Bruce Willis, Ben Affleck, Sylvester Stallone, James Caan and Hugh Heffner. In 2008 the classic 1955 Grand National Show winner, a Chevy Cameo, was signed by a host of Country and Western stars, amongst them Brenda Lee, Phil Everly, the Bellamy Brothers, Kris Kristofferson, Crystal Gayle, Dolly Parton and Olivia Newton John, also to raise funds for the CSN charity.

At Bressingham Steam Gardens, near Diss, Norfok, there is an exhibition based on the popular television series *Dad's Army*. One of the exhibits is an Army jeep which has been signed by many of the actors.

Army jeep signed by some cast members of Dad's Army, on show at Bressingham Steam Museum, Norfolk

Robin Reliant signed by some cast members from Only Fools and Horses, on show at Bressingham Steam Museum, Norfolk

Amongst the signatures are Clive Dunn and script writers Jimmy Perry and David Croft. It's surprising how often you will come across signed vehicles – and other items – in museums and tourist attractions, and just goes to show that wherever you are, a keen autograph hunter should be on watch. Admittedly you can't take these pieces home with you, but often you will be allowed to photograph them, making an interesting adjunct to your collection.

Dad's Army was a television programme screened between 1968 and 1977, which related the adventures of a rather hapless and shambolic Home Guard unit during the Second World War. It was immensely popular, running into eighty episodes as well as a feature film, and its humour plus total lack of bad language made it ideal viewing for all the family. Despite its light-heartedness, it successfully managed to convey aspects of the war – rationing, blackout, air raids, black market – to generations of young people born after the hostilities, and so was a valuable social history document.

The platoon, known as the Walmington-on-Sea Home Guard, was led by Captain Mainwaring played by Arthur Lowe. John Le Mesurier played the rather vague, upper class Sergeant Wilson, while Clive Dunn took the part of an elderly, excitable ex-Boer war soldier, Lance Corporal Jones. Other characters included Private Frazer (James Laurie) Private Walker (Jimmy Beck) Private Godfrey (Arnold Ridley) Private Pike (Ian Lavender) ARP Warden Hodges (Bill Pertwee) and the Vicar (Frank Williams), and they had several catchphrases, notably Jones' 'Don't panic' and 'They don't like it up 'em', and Mainwaring's 'You stupid boy'. In 2000 the Dad's Army Appreciation Society set up a collection of memorabilia at Bressingham Steam Museum, which includes several of the vehicles used in the series notably Jones' butcher's van and an army car. The car has been autographed by many of the actors. There are also room settings and shops.

Also to be seen at Bressingham is a yellow Robin Reliant with 'Trotter's Independent Trading Co.' embellished on the side. This was used in the highly successful series *Only Fools and Horses* which starred David Jason as Del Boy, and Nicholas Lyndhurst as Rodney, and it has been signed by several members of the cast. So it really is worth keeping a look out when you visit museums and similar collections for autographed items such as these, and if photos are allowed they can add depth and appeal to a collection of related names.

Graffiti

Graffiti is nothing new; it was practised in ancient times. The earliest known is a 3,500 year old inscription scratched onto a building near the Sakkara Pyramid in Egypt, which reads: 'I am very impressed by Pharaoh Djoser's pyramid'. Similar graffiti-type inscriptions were found amongst the ruins of Pompeii, and some of the comments were signed, much as we still see today around our towns: 'Lucius painted this,' 'We two dear men, friends forever, were here. If you want to know our names, they are Gaius and Aulus', 'Satura was here on September 3rd' and 'Daphnus was here with his Felicla'. In St Mary's church at Ashwell in Hertfordshire, there are numerous examples of medieval graffiti carvings, amongst them (obviously a comment from a critical workman), 'The corners are not jointed correctly. I spit on them', and, written perhaps by some bored naughty choirboy 'The Archdeacon is an ass'.

It isn't just commoners who vandalised property; royalty did it too. At Woodstock Manor, Oxfordshire, the following has been scratched onto a window by Queen Elizabeth 1 using a diamond:' Much suspected by me, Nothing proved can be, Quoth Elizabeth prisoner.' At the Old Hotel, Buxton, Derbyshire, is another message scratched on a window: 'Buxton, whose warm waters have made the name famous, perchance I shall visit

Graffiti signatures etched onto a window in Leicester's Guildhall

'Tagging' graffiti on a telephone junction box

thee no more 'Farewell'. It was written by Mary, Queen of Scots, in 1573. She was held in the building as a house prisoner by her sister Queen Elizabeth I. Strictly speaking, graffiti isn't an autograph unless it consists of a signature, but it's amazing how many people do include their names, even though there is a possibility they could be in trouble or fined for doing so. Following the Jacobean uprising of 1745, the Redcoats were stationed at Braemar Castle, Deeside, in Scotland, to keep the peace. Several of them, including Ensign B. Sullivan and Corporal William Dix, etched their names onto the castle's walls and window shutters, and the signatures can still be seen. On the shutters in the drawing room are the words 'John Chestnut, Sergeant, 1797'.

The old Elizabethan house in Stratford-upon-Avon where William Shakespeare was born in 1564 has a window upon which many names have been scratched with diamond rings. The tradition apparently began in 1769 when the famous Shakespearean actor David Garrick organised the first Shakespeare festival. Since then it became something of a tradition for literary giants to carve their names on the pane. Amongst the signatures are those of Charles Dickens (1838), John Keats (1817), Mark Twain (1873), Sir Walter Scott (1821) and Thomas Hardy (1896). There are several others, including Tennyson. The window was replaced, but the original glass panes are still on display. There are thousands of windows, walls, pillars and church doors the length and breadth of Britain with old scratched-on signatures, such as a window in the ancient timber framed Leicester Guildhall. In America is a large sandstone cliff, north of the Shoshone River, between Cowley and Byron, in Wyoming. Known as 'Signature Rock', it has been carved with names and dates by adventurous pioneers in the 1800s, corresponding to various crossings of the river. A similar set of carvings still remains on a cliff face near Bridger Creek. In a way, this is a kind of graffiti, too, though this was made with a historic purpose; to record the river crossings of the American settlers as the wagon trains made their long treks across the country into the unknown.

Coming right up to date, the intricate graffiti of our modern decades often consists of 'tagging' – an ornate signature, usually illegible except to those 'in the know'. Often these are signals used by gangs to mark their territory, but sometimes they are practised by a small group or a solitary individual through boredom. Occasionally, the designs are more decorative, and are attempts by the creator to demonstrate his creativity. These signatures can be found everywhere; on walls, hoardings, telephone kiosks, road signs, bridges and lampposts – anywhere a tagger feels he has a good chance of getting an admiring audience. Some examples of modern graffiti are regarded as works of art in their own right, notably those by 'Banksy'.

Banksy, whose real name is unknown, produces elaborate murals, many of them witty or satirical comments of aspects of everyday life. He is believed to have been born near Bristol in 1974, and his work developed in Bristol in the late 1980s, which was the time that many so called 'street artists' discovered the effectiveness and immediacy of the aerosol paint canister. The graffiti works by Banksy usually involve stencils as well as the freehand painting/aerosol designs. His paintings crop up in many places; a giant rat decorates the wall of a public house in Liverpool, a naked man dangles from a window in Bristol and a small boy is depicted fishing in Camden, London. However, much of his work has been erased or painted over by councils who dislike the graffiti works. Even zoos aren't safe – London Zoo had a 7 ft high Banksy message inside the penguin enclosure, 'We're bored of fish', while the elephant enclosure in Bristol Zoo was decorated with, 'I want out. This place is too cold. Keeper smells. Boring, boring, boring.' He produced a quantity of spoof £10 notes in 2004, labelled 'Banksy of England' bearing the head of Princess Diana, which subsequently sold for around £200 each, while a limited edition signed poster which he issued to mark the death of Princess Diana later sold at the London auction house of Bonhams for £24,000.

His most audacious pranks have been to hang his own paintings amongst those exhibited at major art galleries and museums. The British Museum in London one day discovered a Bansky depiction of a primitive painting showing a human figure hunting wildlife whilst pushing a shopping trolley; subsequently they added it to their collection. In the Louvre, in Paris, staff discovered Banksy's version of the Mona Lisa, with a yellow smiley face .

A popular form of graffiti has developed in which underground trains are decorated, sometimes with extraordinarily intricate artworks. Subways and platform walls become targets too. The authorities spend thousands of pounds removing the paint, and have built up an archive of various tags and styles which have enabled them to trace many of the perpetrators. Punishment ranges from large fines to prison sentences. Some youngsters, interrupted while spray painting, fled across the rails into the path of a train and tragically were killed.

Graffiti mural by Banksy in Liverpool

Signed covers and stamp sheets

This fast-growing hobby is fuelled by such companies as Buckingham Covers, who sell attractively-designed covers or FDCs (First Day Covers), signed by famous people from all walks of life. FDCs are envelopes bearing new issues of postage stamps, which have been post-marked with the first date of issue, while other covers bear older stamps related to the featured subject. This is a relatively new way of collecting autographs, and has followed on from the traditional collecting

Buckingham cover signed by Captain Ian McNaught, Master of the QEII and Captain Mike Bannister, Head of Corcorde, carried on board the last ever Concorde flight and the last QEII Blue Riband voyage

theme of stamp collectors who used to buy a first day cover with each new set of stamps issued by Royal Mail. However, according to Buckingham Covers many collectors simply can't keep up with all the stamps now issued by Royal Mail, and sometimes collectors can feel exploited. Consequently, collectors often now choose their subjects of interest, collecting by theme, autograph or just cherry pick anything they like! Popular themes include Concorde, Politics, Films, Football and Victoria Cross winners. Royalty and WW2, though still sought, are not quite so much in demand as they once were.

Buckingham Covers say that autographed covers didn't really exist until the 1960s but have been growing in popularity ever since. Interestingly, you can buy top autographs on covers for much less than on photographs, football shirts etc even though covers are limited editions – because once they are postmarked, no more can be made. Douglas Bader's autograph on a 1965 Biggin Hill cover cost probably around 25p at the time. It now adds over £100 to the cover. Bobby Moore and Alf Ramsey were even more lucrative. Many collectors paid £1 more for the pair and also did the same on the Winners issue. Today, the four covers would cost up to £2,000! Autographs are worth more on relevant covers (where the theme of the cover connects to the person who has signed). Condition is also very important. We also now find autographed stamp sheets (which are numbered limited editions) to be very popular, especially as they frame nicely for the wall. But again, people tend to collect by theme or by what they like.

Tony Buckingham, founder of Buckingham Covers, said that he has raised nearly £500,000 for good causes through signed covers. These will always be limited to the number of covers the celebrity is willing to sign. Since he started, Tony has tried to get the best signatures. It does not always work, but if you aim high, your standards stay high. Tony is proud of the charity work done by his company, and of the great signatures he has obtained for collectors. Glancing through the Buckingham Cover's catalogue, you will find a veritable 'Who's Who' of famous names and you are bound to find some of your favourites there. Not only will you receive an authenticated autograph, you will have the additional enjoyment of an attractive piece of artwork, adorned with beautiful postage stamps. Amongst the featured names are Nelson Mandela, Archbishop Tutu, Sir Bobby Charlton, Sir Geoff Hurst, Jason Robinson, Ben Cohen, Dame Judi Dench, Dame Maggie Smith, Lord Snowden, Felicity Kendall, David Suchet, Sir Terry Wogan, Sir Alan Ayckbourn, Dame Judi Dench and Michael Bond, and there are hundreds more.

Provenance is important. Tony stated that he once saw a great

15TH ANNIVERSARY *of the* CHANNEL TUNNEL - THE OFFICIAL OPENING

Buckingham cover signed by Phillip Cole commemorating the 15th anniversary of the channel tunnel

Montgomery of Alamein cover but it had been signed by his son, not the Field Marshall himself, and was bought by a dealer who was selling it apparently cheaply at £225. In fact, the son's signature is only worth £20. He also tells how Bobby Moore signed many covers while he was alive - and even more it seems, since he passed away! His signature is regularly forged. Tony's advice is that if you buy autographs (on covers or anything else), buy from someone you trust. 'We can all make mistakes but a reputable dealer will put it right.'

The variety of signed first day covers available is amazing, and many of them now change hands for very high prices. So what might you expect to find? The following are all from Buckingham Covers, and include such delights as a British Hedgehog Preservation Society official first day cover signed by Ben Fogel, which was released in 2010. On release, it cost £22.95 and the likely value in the future is unknown as yet. This Hedgehog 'cover' has been hugely popular with cover collectors and hedgehog enthusiasts so it may sell out, which would increase the value long term. The stamps are from a set issued by Royal Mail on 13 April, 2010 called 'British Mammals' Ben Fogel is a relevant autograph as he's a patron of the British Hedgehog Preservation Society. He signed to raise funds for them. An earlier animal issue was the 'Down on the Farm' first day cover signed by author Dick King Smith, which was released in 2005. The stamps were from a set issued by Royal Mail called 'Farm Animals', but they were not the most popular of sets, as the pictures weren't very exciting. Dick King Smith signed a limited number. The tie-in was because he was the author of the children's classic story *The Sheep Pig* (later made into the film *Babe*) and there was a pig on the stamps.

Lord of the Rings; Return of the King Buckingham cover signed by Gandalf, (Sir Ian McKellen) and Saruman (Sir Christopher Lee)

Another children's author is the very popular Michael Bond, and in 2006 he signed the 'Paddington Bear' first day cover, which is now a classic cover. When released it cost £22.95 but four years' later this rose to £35. The stamps are from a set issued by Royal Mail on 10 January, 2006 called 'Animal Tales' which features characters from famous children's books. This cover raised funds for Action Medical Research, and Michael Bond is obviously relevant as he is the creator of Paddington Bear. A popular Paddington Bear signed collectable is a Paddington Bear stamp sheet signed by Michael Bond. Stamp sheets are printed by Royal Mail and include genuine postage stamps but are exclusive to the designer/producer, in this case, Buckingham Covers. This particular sheet

Buckingham cover signed by presenter Ben Fogle

Autographed stamp sheet signed by author Michael Bond

was released in 2008 in partnership with Action Medical Research as a fund raising project, for £24.95, and two years later it was selling at £55.

Autographed stamp sheets are quite a new collectable and exploded in popularity a few years ago, with prices rising very fast. For example, it was not unusual for Buckingham Covers to sell an unsigned edition of a stamp sheet at £19.95 back in 2006 or 2007 and see it re-sell on an internet auction site within days for over £100. Since the recession, this has calmed down a lot. Interest is still strong and prices do rise over time, but in a slower and more realistic way (over months/years rather than days!). New collectors often frame them for the wall while more traditional collectors store them in albums.

The Darwin Anniversary first day cover signed by Robin Knox Johnson and released in 2009 was an official HMS *Beagle* Project first day cover. Robin Knox Johnson is a patron of HMS *Beagle* Project, and the cover bears a set of Darwin Anniversary stamps issued by Royal Mail on 12 February 2009. The unsigned edition is sold out and the signed edition currently retails at £29.95. It's a great autograph and a nice cover. Another attractive cover is one commemorating the 15th Anniversary of the Channel Tunnel signed Philip Cole, released in 2009. Buckingham Covers produce a very popular series of railway covers but signed editions of these are unusual because it is hard to get good, relevant autographs. This is an exception as it marks the 15th anniversary of the Channel Tunnel (postmarked on that date) and is signed by the driver of the Royal Train back in 1994, Phillip Cole. This may well prove a modest investment over time, as railway covers tend to steadily increase over the years.

Not all of the covers are linked to the new releases. Sometimes, a commemorative cover is one that is nothing to do with Royal Mail and does not bear new stamps. Instead, a cover producer like Buckingham Covers decides to commemorate an event or anniversary, sources old stamps to use and sponsors their own postmark (which they design and pay for but Royal Mail apply). This makes them more exclusive and means the date on the postmark has relevance to the event/anniversary/birthday (whereas with a first day cover, the date on the postmark is the day that the new stamps have been issued). For instance, the 2008 Champions League commemorative cover which was produced to mark the 2008 Champions League and Manchester United's win. Signed by Ryan Giggs, it currently retails at £79.95. Only 50 exist, each individually numbered. The cover is part of their popular football series and Buckingham Covers have had all kinds of footballers sign for them.

Some covers are particularly special and have good investment potential, such as the Concorde Last Flight from New York to London commemorative cover signed by Captain Mike Bannister. This was released on the 24 October 2003, and is one of Buckingham Covers' all time best sellers. It sold out within hours of being advertised, had a long waiting list and continues to be the focus of high demand. In fact, the company is continuously trying to buy the cover back from private collections in order to meet the demands of the waiting list. These covers were signed by Mike Bannister, ex Head of Concorde and Pilot of that final Concorde flight, NY-London, and they were officially flown on board. He signed each one, and at the time they sold for £24.95. Now Buckingham covers sell them (when they can buy them back) for £60, and at the peak, they were going much higher than this on the internet

232

auction sites; although Concorde isn't quite as crazily huge as it originally was, it is still a very strong collecting interest.

Another Concorde-linked cover was one commemorating the Last Voyage of QE2 and Last Flight of Concorde, signed by Captain Mike Bannister and Captain Ian McNaught in 2004. Yet again, this proved an all time best seller. One of a limited edition of just 540, this cover honours two 1969 icons: Concorde and QE2. Buckingham Covers worked with British Airways and Cunard to arrange its journeys: the cover was carried onboard the last ever Concorde flight and the last QE2 Blue Riband voyage and genuinely signed by both Captain Mike Bannister (Head of Concorde) and Captain Ian McNaught (Master of the QE2). One of these covers, sold at the pre-issue price of £49.95, resold at auction for £275 within weeks (a good example of why it pays to reserve covers before release). Concorde was also featured on first day cover signed by Chuck Yeager, the first man to break the sound barrier. Released on 2 May 2002, this was a hard autograph to get, and sold out at the time at the price of £75. Today, they would sell them at £200, but it is one you just never see, as they are all in private collections.

A good collectable is the *Harry Potter and the Goblet of Fire* first day cover from the Isle of Man signed by Ralph Fiennes. Ralph Fiennes is a notoriously hard autograph to get so Buckingham Covers were thrilled when he agreed to sign just fifty of the Harry Potter cover (Ralph Fiennes plays Lord Voldemort, the ultimate baddie, in the films) to raise funds for UNICEF. The cover sold out pre-release and cost £50 at the time. Today, they would cost double, but they never seem to come up for sale. Harry Potter of course is another collecting theme that appeals to a big fan base, not just cover collectors. Also with a film theme is a superb James Bond first day cover signed by Sir Roger Moore and released on 8 January 2009. James Bond covers were particularly successful as they appealed to James Bond fans from all over the world as well as cover collectors, and Buckingham Covers had a large selection of Bond autographed editions, most of which sold out. This one signed by Sir Roger Moore (James Bond of course!) was very popular and was signed to raise funds for UNICEF.

Film themes seem well sought-after. A Lord of the Rings New Zealand double first day cover was signed by Sir Ian McKellen and Sir Christopher Lee to raise money for the Great Ormond Street children's hospital's Children's Charity. Sir Ian played a big part in bringing the total that was raised through celebrity signed covers to £32,000. The pictures on this cover are genuine New Zealand stamp sheets. Each stamp sheet is postmarked in New Zealand (where the *Lord of the Rings* trilogy was filmed) on the dates the films were released. One stamp sheet shows Sir Ian McKellen as Gandalf and the other shows Sir Christopher Lee as Saruman. The cover itself is a limited edition of 300 of which just twenty were double signed by both McKellen and Lee. These again sold out pre-release at the price of £99.95 and it is unlikely it will be possible to buy any back in the future as the price of these will rise.

One of the jewels is the 25th Anniversary of the Falklands Conflict commemorative cover signed by the Duke of Edinburgh, released on 5 April 2007. Ellie of Buckingham covers explains: The Duke of Edinburgh is one who basically never signs. The Queen has never signed and it is almost unheard of that her husband has. But he agreed to sign fifty of Buckingham Covers' Falklands commemorative cover to raise funds for the Falkland Islands Memorial Chapel (we've raised over £20,000 for them). These sold out pre-release and are never seen to buy back but if they were, the price would be around £495. They sold for £300 at the time with a waiting list of collectors who missed out. Another best seller is the official TV Times first day cover signed by the Two Ronnies; Ronnie Barker and Ronnie Corbett. Collectors fell over themselves to own this cover when five hundred covers were released in 2005. The double signed edition sold out overnight. Within a week or so, Ronnie Baker passed away. As is the horrible way with signed covers, there was a rush of new collectors wanting covers autographed by Ronnie Barker after his death. But it was too late! They were sold out to regular collectors. This is another cover which is rarely seen or available to buy back. If it was, it would probably now be sold for about £150. The pre-release price was £23.95 in 2005 so how is that for an investment?'

Buckingham cover signed by the Duke of Edinburgh

CHAPTER TWELVE

Family history, the history of writing and how to store autographs

IF YOU ARE one of the thousands of people researching your family history, then autographs are very special things to find. They are immensely personal items, and knowing that one of your long-departed ancestors once touched that very piece of paper, gives a strange feeling of continuity. It's also intriguing to try to spot if you have 'inherited' certain handwriting quirks,; maybe the formation of a letter 'S', or a distinctive dotting of an 'I'.

Cards and Documents

I was once clearing out a cupboard, and right at the back I found a carrier bag of old Christmas cards. I was about to throw them away when something stopped me. I remembered that I had given the cards, dating from around twenty years ago, to my children when they were small so that they could use them in their scrapbooks. On looking through the cards, I realised that many bore signatures of relatives since deceased – here were grandparents, aunts, uncles, and cousins who would never sign their names again. Not only was it a trip down memory lane, it was a salutary reminder that even the most ubiquitous of items can prove to be a valuable item to the genealogist seeking family treasures. I then began searching through other items which I had ferreted away, and was thrilled to discover several postcards written by my grandfather in the 1950s, as well as some penned by other relatives. These were swiftly moved to my 'family tree album'.

Official documents are an excellent source of finding ancestors'

A book signing by author/illustrator Jennifer Ruby, 1980s

signatures, especially if you can obtain the originals; I have a marriage certificate signed by my great great grandparents in 1844, not long after the official registration certificates were first introduced, in 1837. However, remember that hand-written copies which are obtained later from the records office will not bear the original signatures of your relatives, just those of the clerk who copied the certificate. To see the original signatures, if you don't have the certificate given to the couple at the time, you need to find the register that the couple signed at the church in which they married.

It is possible however, to see signatures earlier than 1837 by looking at such items as baptismal records – that way I found the signature of my great great great grandfather, dated 1799 – while if your ancestors signed wills, deeds or bonds, then these will all bear their writing. Of course, if they couldn't write, and many people were still illiterate even in the late 1800s, then it will bear their mark, probably an 'X'. Interestingly, the census for 1911 has been scanned from the originals, so if you look up your ancestors on this, you can see not only their actual signature but the names of their wives and children, occupations, ages and other information, all in your ancestor's own handwriting, which is very exciting and shows the style he used.

I inherited an old metal box which had once belonged to my great grandfather, and then was passed down to one of his sons. The box was a treasure trove. It contained letters dating from the 1870s, written by one of his daughters who had emigrated to Australia, a bundle of returned cheques from the early 1900s, a 1900s rent book, a letter sent in 1870 to my great great grandmother from a son aboard a merchant vessel en route to San Francisco via China, and a beautiful card, written in copperplate by my great grandfather, containing birth dates and christenings of all his eleven siblings. All of these things are of interest to the autograph collector, especially one who is also tracing the family tree. In addition, there was a bundle of greetings cards, visiting cards, 'In Memoriam' cards and black-edged letters of sympathy. Practically every item bore a signature, mainly in attractively formed ink handwriting, such a contrast to today's ballpoint scrawls.

Family Bibles often record events such as births, marriages and deaths.

Signature on a family Bible 1869

I am lucky enough to have one of these which lists a few names. However, the one once owned by my great great grandfather which passed down to a cousin, is full of names and dates in exquisite hand writing – such a shame we seem to have lost the knack – letting us see just how beautiful his lettering was. It's so obvious that, decades ago, many hours must have been devoted at school to the teaching of handwriting and to the formation of letters. In those days, people were encouraged to write beautifully, using elaborate sweeps and swirls. People took pride in their writing, not just 'best' writing, but in everyday tasks. The changing appearance of autograph books, from the neat, pleasing books of the late nineteenth and early twentieth centuries, to the looser hand of the 1940s and fifties, and though the scrawl of the 1960s onwards, is interesting though rather sad.

Quilts and samplers

Though not strictly autographical, samplers are another means of 'writing' a name by embroidering it onto a piece of fabric. Samplers were made by very young girls, often under the age of ten. Although the skilfulness of the stitching varies, many of them are exquisite, using tiny stitches to

Victorian and Edwardian family memorabilia, all bearing signatures

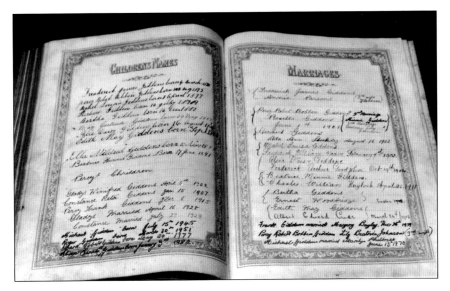

Family Bible with many inscriptions

create complex designs. The earliest samplers are thought to have appeared in the fifteenth century, and originally were a quick way of recording various patterns which could then be incorporated in large embroideries. The earliest documented sampler evidence appeared in a household expenses account of Elizabeth of York, wife of Henry VII in 1502 and the earliest known signed and dated sampler was made by Jane Bostocke, who dated her work 1598. The sampler can be seen in the Victoria and Albert Museum, (V&A), in London.

Gradually, samplers came to resemble those seen in museums today – complex pieces of embroidery depicting alphabets, pictures and patterns. Usually they also bear the name of the person who sewed the sampler and a date, though sometimes they just have initials or are anonymous. By the nineteenth century, schoolgirls were producing samplers to show their proficiency in sewing; maybe they were allowed to produce these beautiful things as a reward for doing well in their plain sewing (repairing, darning and making basic garments). Later, though, samplers became less intricate and were more like examples of basic techniques such as buttonholing, hemming and darning; practical rather than pretty. By then, the sewing machine was common and intricate sewing techniques were becoming unfashionable. Nowadays, with the huge interest in embroidery, samplers are being sewn by women once more for decorative reasons. Vectis sold a delightful embroidered sampler

Sampler worked by a 7 year-old girl in 1837

signed by A Johnson, aged seven, in 1837. This sampler, on a cream linen ground, was worked with letters of the alphabet, numbers, flowers, acorns, birds, animals and a short quote, ' *A good Education is a great Blessing*' and sold for £80. Another, more intricate, silk and chenille sampler reached £2,500. This piece of embroidery was produced by Grace Evanes dated 1830 from Caernarvon '*In Grace Jones Williams' School*'. The complicated design included a large running stag, three fully rigged ships and a wide floral border. It's difficult to imagine a young girl today having the talent or the staying power to create such a beautiful item.

Another form of needlework which involves names is the sewing of signature quilts, sometimes known as 'friendship quilts'. Particularly popular in America, they were sometimes created in Britain, too, and basically consist of patchwork quilts or hangings in which some or all of the squares have blank spaces for a name or signature to be entered. Sometimes the signature was inked, usually in a permanent or 'indelible' type of ink, and sometimes it was embroidered over in a coloured thread to tone with the pattern on the quilt. These quilts date back to the early 1800s, and occasionally, as well as names, they would contain poems or biblical texts.

The quilts were made for various reasons, including fundraising. During America's Civil war, women raised money to help the soldiers by charging fees for the privilege of having a signature incorporated onto a square of a quilt. Eventually, the quilt would contain hundreds of signatures and then be raffled, so that the money raised from the sale could be added to the money raised from the selling of the squares. In this way, large sums could be accumulated. Often, though, the quilts were made as friendship declarations – maybe a group of friends who enjoyed patch-working would each contribute signed samples of their work, which they then sewed together. Another reason the quilts were made was to commemorate a special event such as a wedding, birth, birthday or anniversary.

As autograph collecting became more popular, in the mid 1800s, so

240

some women and girls began making quilts with written or embroidered thoughts and signatures upon the squares, rather like a fabric autograph album. This is something which keen needle-workers could do today, making permanent autograph collections but getting their friends to sign cloth squares which could then be sewn together to use as quilts or cushion covers. I have heard of people signing tablecloths, and then the cloth's owner embroiders over every name, giving a beautiful permanent reminder of a group of friends. Not so much practised now is the signing of handkerchiefs. At one time, the handkerchief was a vital piece of everyone's dress, but then along came the tissue. Monogrammed handkerchiefs were very popular, but also found are hankies signed with autographs, as keepsakes, probably a cheaper version of the 'sign a tablecloth' event as mentioned above (or maybe one to carry out if you didn't have many friends!).

History of writing

Long ago, people couldn't write because the concept was unknown. Maybe they scratched symbols in the mud or dust, signs which informed their friends that they had passed by. How did people learn to write, and why was it necessary? Writing developed over thousands and thousands of years. Before people had devised a way of communicating through 'writing', they drew pictures to explain their feelings or to leave messages. Cave dwellers in prehistoric times made drawings on the cave walls to show animals they had hunted, sometimes telling the story of the hunt over a series of pictures. The Ancient Egyptians used pictures to record information and to communicate too. Of course, the drawback with pictures was that not everything could be depicted in this way – names, for instance, or thoughts or dates – while, because drawings could be interpreted in many different ways, you could never be sure that the message you were trying to transmit would be correctly understood. In Egypt, the pictures gradually developed into Hieroglyphs, a form of picture writing where the pictures were somewhat simplified. This was a sacred form of writing, used to record important information about religion or the pharaoh, and written on the walls of the temples, or maybe tombs. Gradually, hieroglyphic signs developed into Hieratic which was easier to write. In turn, Hieratic morphed into Demotic, which was even faster to write, and this form of script became used for official documents.

Many different kinds of scripts emerged as communities developed across the world. The first people to depict the vowels as symbols were the Greeks, and languages such as Arabic, Cyrillic and Latin were based on

The Rosetta Stone

the Greek alphabet, and they were honed and refined until today where basic symbols allow us to communicate quickly and easy, whatever our language.

Early peoples wrote their messages on stone, bone, or clay tablets. Other materials used were leather, linen or ivory. Papyrus was developed by the Egyptians. This was a kind of paper made from the fibres of the reeds growing alongside the Nile, and in turn, this was replaced by parchment. Various inks were created which were suited to write on these new, softer materials, and which were so much easier and quicker than chisels and styluses. Several kinds of cloth were also used, the most famed of the ancient cloth writings being the Dead Sea scrolls, written by the Essenes and hidden in clay pots in a cave. Two thousand years after they had been secreted away, they were rediscovered, demonstrating some of the earliest documentation of Judaism.

> *In 1799 one of Napoleon's soldiers discovered a large stone covered with symbols, which we now refer to as the Rosetta Stone after the town in which it was found. This stone was invaluable to the research of scientists, notably Jean-Francoise Champollion, who finally made the deciphering of hieroglyphs break through in 1822. People had striven for hundreds of years to make sense of the hieroglyphic language; now, suddenly, the 'code' was broken.*

Ink

Ancient cultures used ink and would have independently formulated their own techniques to enable them to write or to draw. Usually the inks were made from plant dyes, berries, minerals such as graphite, or from animal matter including squids and cochineal beetles. Other substances used included soot, tar, pitch, burnt bones, twigs, plant galls and roots. These would all be pounded or ground, mixed with water, glue, oil, gelatine or

"Has my young brother fallen in the Ink?"

Judith Beedle
August 2[...] 19[...]

243

other thinners or thickeners depending on the consistency, and binders, then strained. Recipes include one, which first became popular around one thousand five hundred years ago, which consisted of iron salts and tannins (obtained from galls), mixed together with a thickener to create a blue-black ink. Over time, this faded to brown. The Ancient Greeks and Romans often used a substance made from soot, glue and water while medieval scribes used an ink made from the hammered bark of hawthorn branches, soaked for a period of time in water, then boiled and mixed with wine and iron salt. By the twelfth century, ink was a mixture of ferrous sulphate, gum, gall and water, but once the printing press had been developed by Johannes Gutenberg in the fifteenth century, a thick, oily, ink was used which enabled it to adhere to the printing surfaces. Unfortunately, the iron and gall ink developed in the Middle Ages, and used by such people as Leonardo de Vinci, Rembrandt, Bach, Handel and Charles Dickens is now proving something of a threat to old manuscripts. The iron sulphate has started to react with the surface of the paper, making it brittle, and so conservationists and archivists are battling to salvage these historic documents.

Modern inks are chemical based and part of a complex industry. They tend to be made from such things as carbon black, a heavy varnish, plus a drier. They are many different types and consistencies, depending on the type of pen or the application. Some inks are thick and black, while others are pale and watery. Indian ink, a thick black ink beloved of artists and which is often seen in drawings in autograph books, is a mixture of carbon, gum Arabic, borax, shellac and camphor.

Writing Implements

At first, people drew with the nearest thing to hand – literally, They used their fingers which they dipped in plant juices or dyes to depict their works, or scratched them onto stones and rocks with sharp flints, bones or bronze tools. Early Egyptians used reeds of bamboo or calamus (a sweet flag with thick stems which grows near riverbanks), while the Chinese made brushes using hairs from rats or camels to create their sweeping, stylised drawings and lettering.

European monks experimented and discovered that quill pens made from goose feathers worked better than reeds, because the hollow quill held the ink and by splitting the end, a nib was formed. The thickness of the stroke was easier to control too. Quills were used for hundreds of years, but they had drawbacks. They constantly needed trimming, and the life of a quill wasn't long as they soon split. Even so, beautiful illuminated bibles, as well as books from great novelists such as Jane Austin and

Charlotte Bronte, would have been written using quills.

> *Quill pens were introduced around 700 AD, and the most common were made from goose feathers. The best quills were made from the five outer left wing feathers, which had been taken from living birds in the spring. The left wing was preferred because when used by a right-handed person the feathers curved outwards and away from their face. Although goose quills were the most common, other feathers were used too; the most expensive were swan which were considered a higher grade. For fine lines, crow, hawk, owl, turkey and other birds were used. There were many drawbacks with the quill, notably the time taken to trim and prepare the nib and they had to be replaced after a week, so unlike the later dip pen, they proved expensive.*

Then came a revolution – steel pen nibs. These were patented by Bryan Donkin, an English engineer, in 1803, but he didn't commercially exploit his patent, and so in the 1830s steel nibs began to be mass produced in Birmingham. Metal nibs could be fitted to quills, and also to handles made from wood or metal. These so-called 'dip pens' remained in use for the next hundred years or so – even in the 1950s children were being

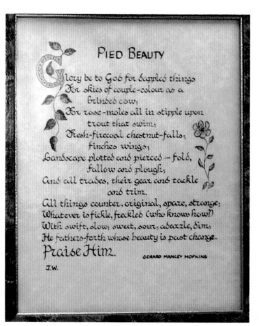

Example of modern calligraphy

taught to write with these pens before graduating to fountain pens. Certainly, during the 1950s many head teachers considered that a dip pen was essential to teach a child the correct formation of the letters; a child could 'feel' the shape of the letters more so than with the fountain pen. The fountain pen was allowed when the child could produce a piece of handwriting in the school's chosen style. I recall that once we were proficient with our dip pens when I was at primary school in the 1950s, our headmaster suggested to parents that they buy us an Osmiroid pen with an italic nib. This pen, in his opinion, was easiest to use, good value for money, and could be used to produce a neat style as decreed by London Schools Inspector Marion Richardson (see below) even though it was fitted with the italic nib. At that time, a headmaster's words were considered law, so naturally we all saved our pocket money to buy an Osmiroid pen. Mine was bright green, and I was so proud of it.

Fountain pens, which now can be either refillable or take ink cartridges, surprisingly date back to 953 when Ma'ad al-Mu'izz of Egypt was given a pen with an ink-filled reservoir, which reached the nib via capillary action. However, in modern times, the pens weren't really in regular use until the early 1900s. Lewis Waterman created a pen in 1884 which contained an efficient capillary action, utilising a feed with conduits to guide the ink down the back of the nib to the paper but a problem with these early pens was leakage, and makers such as Parker Pens were continually striving to improve the performance. In 1894 Parker invented a system known as the 'lucky curve' to drain the ink back into the reservoir when the pen wasn't being used. Early pens were called 'eyedroppers' because they had to be filled each day with a dropper, but gradually, as more innovations were made, pens were filled by more reliable methods such as the piston, the lever and, later, the cartridge.

Today, most of us write using a ballpoint pen. These pens are quick and easy to use, they don't need to be constantly refilled with ink, and are cheap so can be discarded when they run dry. Although a patent on a ballpoint pen was issued in 1888, they didn't go into commercial production till Laszlo Biro took out an improved patent in 1943. Ballpoint pens work by the means of a small ball which picks up an oil based ink, stimulated as the pen is moved over the paper. The 1960s saw the introduction of the felt tip pen, and roller ball pens appeared in the 1980s. Similar to a ballpoint, the roller ball uses a liquid ink which gives a smoother flow of ink. Many celebrities nowadays sign their autographs with gel pens, marker pens or highlighters, as these are often available in eye-catching metallic or sparkly ink, which enhances their signature.

Writing styles

One of the most fascinating things about autograph collecting is noting how people's handwriting styles vary so much. This is especially apparent in the autograph albums in which folk have written poems and quotes in their usual style of writing. In contrast, a celebrity, knowing that he will be required to sign his name many times, might well alter his usual signature

Early hornbooks

to make it more attractive, arty or quicker to write. Over time people's handwriting styles tend to change slightly in any case, which is why comparison between signatures often shows variations. This also explains the reason why some so-called 'fake' signatures are not fakes, but just produced at a different period during the lifetime of a celebrity.

In Britain, unlike many other countries, there is no set handwriting style. Schools are free to use various methods, customarily decided on by the head teacher or the member of staff who teaches handwriting. In 1982, the Home Office undertook a project to study handwriting in schools, and to investigate the way in which it was taught. Usually children are first taught to write in capital letters before learning the lower case letters. They are then taught how to join them up although sometimes the 'print script' is adopted and used even in adult life, as a handwriting style in its own right, while some schools teach a print style as a regular form of handwriting. In the eighteenth and nineteenth centuries, most children were taught Copperplate writing, which was a neat, round style with flowing loops, but later, most copybooks switched to Looped Cursive handwriting. This was a style devised by Vere Foster in 1868 for the benefit of Irish emigrants to America, and was still elegant but didn't need such careful precision with nib pressure and thick and thin strokes. It proved very popular with British schools, and was widely used for several decades.

In 1935 Marion Richardson introduced a round hand style of writing which joined up most letters, but without using loops or curls. The most distinctive characters in this script are an open letter 'b' and 'p' and a long 'f'. This is the style which I was taught, and which thousands of other school children learned in the post war years. I well remember long hours spent copying verses from cards that were written in the Marion Richardson hand, to practise the style. Most of the cards seemed to feature the 'Ducks Ditty' poem from the Kenneth Grahame's *The Wind in the Willows*. Nowadays, the round hand system is the style most commonly taught in primary schools, though the open letters are usually dropped, and adapted to a closed style. Running alongside the Marion Richardson style was the Italic hand, which was the 'spiky' kind of writing used at the time of the Italian Renaissance, and which was revived in 1932. In the 1950s, it was adopted by many schools as it was a more elegant and traditional style than the Marion Richardson round writing. This attractive style seems slower to write than a round hand, as it doesn't flow so easily, and therefore is more likely to become messy when rushed. It doesn't seem so popular nowadays.

Today, many people are discovering the art of calligraphy, producing exquisite documents and art works, executed in a careful hand, reminiscent of those manuscripts of a much earlier era. Usually these are produced with modern inks and writing implements, though sometimes people try to make them as authentic as possible by using vellum, quills, gold leaf and rich pigments. Calligraphy is an exciting skill to learn, a direct link with those monks who toiled for years to produce such treasured Bibles, long before the printing press was invented.

What can handwriting tell us?

Many people are convinced that the study of handwriting (graphology) can reveal a person's character. A trained eye can interpret a signature or passage written in an autograph book, and produce an analysis of the writer and his personality. Nevertheless, even without training it is often possible to observe tell-tale signs; from the formation of the letters we can usually deduce whether the writer was young or old, and if he was frail. According to Aristotle, writing in 330 B.C, 'Handwriting is the visible form of speech', and many other prominent people in history professed beliefs

Signed drawing by Nick Parkes

in the connection between handwriting and personality, amongst them William Shakespeare, Carl Jung and Albert Einstein.

If this is the case, then autograph books can reveal a multitude of secrets. We may even be able to analyse our relatives' character traits and foibles by a quick peek at the way they wrote 'By hook or by crook' or 'I will plant a forget-me-not and see if it will grow' all those years ago. There were our relatives, who were just assuming they were kindly bestowing their words of wisdom on the owner of the book, and then all those years later we come along, study their writing and announce they were frauds, or mean-spirited, or aggressive! How can handwriting reveal our secrets? Many people believe that, because the brain guides the hand as it writes, the writing reveals the emotions, thoughts and experiences which are all part of the brain.

Firstly, you need to look at the baseline – autograph books are perfect for this as they rarely have lined paper. Graphologists prefer to analyse handwriting on plain, rather than lined paper, as it is easier to read the characteristics when the writing is not being artificially controlled by the lines. Baselines can be slanted, wavy, straight or erratic. If the baseline is very straight, it can mean that the writer is very tense, or maybe a control-freak, though if it is more-or-less level, then that is quite usual and shows a balanced personality. A very wavy baseline can indicate someone of extreme emotions, while a rising baseline means optimism. In contrast, a descending baseline can mean pessimism or tiredness. Or it could mean that the writer was bored with writing in lots of autograph books!

The handwriting might be vertical, or perhaps slope either right or left. Vertical handwriting indicates a writer whose head rules his heart, someone who attempts to keep their emotions hidden. A slant to the right will often be seen in the handwriting of one who is warm, friendly and caring, while a backwards slant is that of a writer trying to hide their emotions, and who may be cold, shy or indifferent. Size matters, too – large handwriting tends to show that the writer is confident, friendly and outgoing, while small writing can mean the opposite, but might also show the writer is very thoughtful. Heavy strokes which seem almost gouged into the paper, can indicate stress, though if the strokes are just thick but not deeply pressed, then the writer will probably be clear headed, serious, and could be prone to bouts of temper. Very light strokes belong to someone with little physical energy, they may be lethargic or tired, and may also be very sensitive. Average strokes belong to average people with average emotions and stress levels.

People who leave large spaces between their words need plenty of breathing space, they don't want to feel too involved with other people, but very small spaces show someone with a desire to be with others. Extra long strokes on letters such as 'f', 't', 'h' and 'l' can indicate someone with great ambitions, while large lower loops on letters indicate creativity and an artistic nature. A lower stroke which is 'cradle-shaped' can suggest an avoidance of confrontation. Apparently, large upper loops can indicate that the writer is rather head-in-the-clouds – or even slightly crazy. Straight strokes on 'p' and 'g' reveal impatience, while full loops show energy. If the straight stroke of your 't' is at the top, then you're far-seeing, but a wavy stroke shows a flirty nature. A downward stroke can show someone rather domineering. The middle zone of writing – the letters such as 'a', 'e', 'o', 'c' and 'm', which are of uniform height – can be particularly revealing. If the letters are very humped in shape, rather than like that taught when you first learn to write, it can indicate trustworthy, loyal people, though they might be secretive and stubborn, too. An opposite style has the 'n's and 'm's more like troughs, and these troughs are seen as holders where troubles can be poured. The person who uses this style is likely to be helpful and caring. Pointed letters can be the sign of inquisitiveness while wavy loose, not properly formed handwriting often belongs to a dreamer or an artistic person.

Mounted photograph and autographs of The Beatles

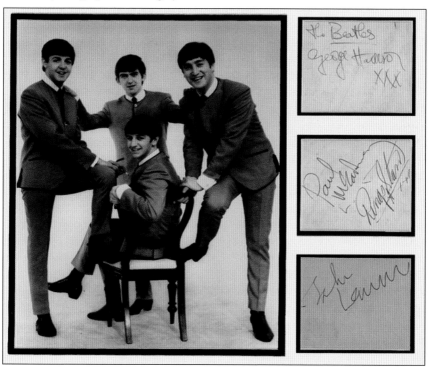

Of course, all this has to approached with caution. When we write a letter of importance - maybe to our employer or someone in authority - we tend to use our best writing, but a note or a shopping list is much more likely to be scrawled. We all know that our handwriting can vary tremendously; if we have been ill or have a pain in our hand or our hand is very cold, then our writing will look shaky and frail. If we use an unfamiliar pen, or one which is threatening to 'dry up', then that will affect the way we write, while if we happen to be balancing the pad on our knees, or are in a bad light, or sitting an a strange angle, then all this will influence how our writing appears. Although certain characteristics, such as the way we form our letters, may remain the same, our writing will still appear different. It is worth bearing this in mind before we dismiss an autograph as 'a fake' because it does not conform to the usual version of a person's signature. It could just be that they were having an off day, or couldn't find anything on which to lean the autograph book.

Where and how should we store our precious collection?

As with any collectable when it comes to storage you need to be very careful. Most autographs are written on paper; in an autograph book, on a letter, a cover or a photograph, and there is a real danger of causing irreversible damage to your collection by not storing the items properly. The first thing to remember is probably the most obvious – store in a dry place. Water, damp and condensation are paper's worst enemies. Heat and sunshine aren't far behind – they make paper brittle and crumbly, while too much light or sun will cause ink to fade. Excessive handling should be avoided as our skin contains oils which react with paper and ink, and ideally, certainly with the more valuable items in your collection, you should always wear thin white cotton gloves when handling them. Another enemy of paper and of books is the insect world. All types of grubs, bugs and flies enjoy nothing better than a munch through a few sheets of paper, or perhaps a feast on the paste used to attach the cover of an autograph album. They might even enjoy a nibble of the cover itself, especially if it's made from a natural fibre or substance, such as silk, linen or leather. Sometimes the insects don't mean to have strayed into the book, but they creep between the pages and get squashed – this often happens with midges, fruit flies, thunder-bugs and the like. So the moral is to ensure that when you read the books, there are no insects around, and when you put them away you cover them or wrap them in tissue. I prefer to keep my autograph books tissue wrapped in cardboard boxes, but many people say that cardboard is harmful as dyes used in the manufacture can leech into the paper.

Whatever you do, be careful how you store autograph books. Don't squash them onto a shelf, ensure each book has room to breathe, and when you remove a book from the shelf try to ensure that you don't pull it by the spine. Most old autograph books have delicate spines which are often already crumbling and splitting due to so much handling. If you store your autographs in envelopes or folders they need to be made from acid free paper or card. Normal paper contains acid from the manufacturing process that will yellow and destroy the paper and print over time. If you do wrap autograph books in tissue paper, make sure that it is acid free, too, and always use white tissue as the dye can leach from the coloured kinds. Autographs shouldn't be stored with newspaper or magazine clippings, as these have a high acid content, nor should they be stored with other kinds of printed, photocopied or typewritten materials because ink and toner can be transferred to the autograph document. Folded letters should be removed from the envelopes and flattened between sheets of acid-free paper or in a sheet protector, because over time the folds can deteriorate and crumble, but be very careful with brittle documents. Always remove staples, paperclips, paper fasteners and other types of metal clips from autograph letters or documents, because they will rust and the rust stains will damage the autograph. Take care if using ring binders or metal clipped binders for storage, as the autographs can rub against the metal and be harmed. Don't try to repair damaged autographs because it is so easy to ruin an autograph and cause it to lose its value. The worst thing you can do is to use sticky, self-adhesive tape, which easily stains documents. Always seek professional advice from a qualified restorer.

Plastic leaves and holders must be carefully chosen, as the plasticisers and coatings on many types of plastics will react with inks in a very short time. Many of the cheap plastic folders and pockets are made from polyvinyl chloride (PVC), which contains plasticisers and is therefore harmful. The excellent Library of Congress website (see appendix) gives plenty of information on storage and preservation, and explains that the ideal material for the long term storage of items such as autographs and covers is uncoated polyester film, although uncoated cellulose triacetate, polyethylene, and polypropylene are also suitable. They can then be housed in paper folders, albums or boxes.

Many people like to display framed autographs, often mounted together with a relevant photograph, letter or press cutting. Having framed autographs on display means that you can easily enjoy them, and providing it is done correctly, won't normally cause harm. However, they should be framed professionally, and be mounted on acid-free, archival quality materials. A special conservation glass should be used, which will keep most of the harmful ultraviolet light away from the framed item, but even this glass does not filter out all ultraviolet rays. Therefore, hang framed autographs away from direct sunlight direct and other bright light, and also away from fluorescent lights which emit ultraviolet rays. It's also not advisable to hang the framed autographs above fireplaces, radiators and other heat sources, or in places where there are extremes of temperatures or humidity, or on outside walls which can often absorb cold and dampness. Aim for a stable, cool and dry environment away from windows.

Autographs often come under the heading 'Ephemera' and the *Shorter Oxford Dictionary* definition of this is: 'Things of short lived use. Lasting or living only for a few days. Transitory.' Hopefully, this book has demonstrated that, far from being transitory, autographs are things to treasure. They are bound up with memories, events and people who have a special meaning for us. By committing their signature and their sentiment to a page, they leave a part of their life in our care. Whether you decide to invest in celebrities and notable people, or prefer to collect the everyday autograph albums filled with the rhymes and drawings of folk you have probably never heard of, autographs make great collectables. When you obtain a signature, you get so much more than a squiggle of ink on paper; you acquire a fragment of that person's existence. Autographs are very personal collectables. They are special and every single one is unique. A one-off signature. What could be more limited, or more distinctive, than that?

APPENDIX I

Useful things to remember when buying autographs

ALWAYS BUY FROM a reputable dealer. If the autograph seems too cheap to be true, then it probably is. Fakes abound, and especially crop up on internet auctions such as Ebay, where anyone can advertise without any form of guarantee. If possible, examine before you buy, and if this isn't possible, ensure that the dealer will take back the autograph if you are not satisfied, without quibbling. Familiarise yourself with your chosen field; get to learn what is available, read up the subject, not just about the handwriting style of the person whose autograph you want, but the kind and colour of ink he uses. Find out the kind of documents he signs, and whether he always puts his autograph in a certain place on the page or photo. If you are after the signature of a 1930s' star, be suspicious if it is signed in ballpoint pen ink, as the pens weren't invented then. Likewise, a 1940s' icon wouldn't use a metallic marker. Complete names are better than just first names. Occasionally you might come across a photo or card which a star had intended for a friend. Therefore, it's unlikely the star would have used his surname.

Always buy from a credited, recognised dealer. AFTAL (Autograph Fair Trade Association Limited) has a list of dealers it recommends (See Appendix II). Autographs may rise in value – but they may equally go down. Celebrities rise and fade, and, for various reasons, may become *persona non gratis* or just fade away into nothingness. Just because you know that an autograph is of a famous person, it may not be as collectable as the seller claims. The paper on which it's written may be discoloured, spotted, stained with sticky tape, water blotched, torn, crumbling away round the edges, creased, bent or worn away. The signature might be smudged, faint or pencilled, whilst often old signatures were written in an acidic, corrosive ink, which gradually eats away at the paper they are written on.

You can find old autographs anywhere, so keep an open mind and always be on the lookout. Try searching antique stores, flea markets, car boot fairs, collectors' outlets, charity shops or even rummaging through your attic. Almost certainly, though, you will have to contact dealers in autographs, auction companies or those sellers of rare books who deal in signatures and signed books. Remember, you get what you pay for, so be prepared to pay well, if you want something special.

Dave Tomlinson of the Laurel and Hardy Society has compiled the following guide. Though some of the advice concerns the autographs of Laurel and Hardy, much of it is common sense which is relevant to any autographs or autograph collectors.

• Laurel and Hardy autographs are in the top echelon of autograph collecting with genuine autographs commanding high market prices. Sadly, there are many out there who want to make a fast buck by selling forgeries as genuine. This advice is offered in order to reduce your chances of buying a forgery, to enjoy your hobby more and to protect your investment.

• Buy from an established reputable source who will offer you guarantees that if, at a later date the item is doubted, you can seek a refund. This could be from a UACC accredited dealer (where his reputation is most important to his business) or from an established expert in the field. Alternatively, buy from someone who can offer credible provenance to the item that can maybe also be verified (e.g. place/date of a theatrical engagement). Avoid low reputation or privately registered sellers on internet auctions. I would however recommend that you do not buy material that is marginal in the sense that there are any doubts in the authenticity (e.g. abnormalities in the signing and uncertainties in the provenance). Those doubts will always remain and will affect the investment when you later want to sell.

• Examine the item thoroughly before buying (or immediately after buying if guarantees provided). You should check that the media is of the correct vintage (i.e. over fifty years old) and that the autographs are neither pre-printed nor rubber-stamped. The surface ink can be checked under a strong light to ensure that the autograph is not part of the photograph and the ink flow can be checked under a magnifying glass.

• Always attempt to seek provenance to the item. That is, where/when the item was signed and the story behind it; this adds credibility, interest and much more value. Don't be fooled by Certificates of Authenticity (COAs). These add very little value, can be misleading, and generally seek to give undue credibility. They are little more than someone else's opinion through comparing with a few exemplars and are often provided where doubts exist. However, always check sellers' guarantees.

• Do your homework and become familiar with the following with regard to stars like Laurel and Hardy:

• The shape of their autograph including letter shapes, typical characteristics in their flourishes and the application of pen drops. Ollie often dotted his 'i' and Stan usually put a full stop at the end of his name.

• Pen types and colours. Before 1947 they would use classical dark blue/black fountain pen ink. Post 1947 Stan occasionally used biro to sign autograph books but always preferred his fountain pen. Ollie more liberally used biro including its application to photos. Ollie's ink, including his application of biro to photographs, does have a greater propensity to fade with time. Be very careful of signings where the ink appears to be the same; many forgeries have been done using the same pen. Stan and Ollie were always prepared to sign autographs and each was always armed with their own personal pens. They would certainly not pass the same pen around when mobbed by fans!

• Stan's salutations and their handwriting characteristics. It was common for Stan to inscribe to the recipient with a salutation like 'Hello Sue!' or variations of the less common 'Our best wishes always Sue!' Ollie very rarely wrote an inscription, and really only to his friends and family.

• Signing styles. Stan and Ollie were classical signers with fast flowing, evenly stroked, autographs. Many forgeries appear slowly drawn or even traced that show quivery jaggies and also breaks in the writing. Neither of the boys adopted a calligraphic hand writing style, so beware of autographs that have variations in the thickness of the strokes.

• Signing medium. Stan and Ollie normally signed their own give-away portrait publicity material, autograph books, UK theatrical tour programs or ad-hoc improvised material (eg envelopes, note paper). They very rarely signed film stills or press stills, and if these are seen one should always question the opportunity for them to sign such material.

Stan would often stick a small blue framed vignette sticker, which depicted a caricature of them, to autograph books.

• Placement of autograph on the medium. Stan and Ollie always signed away from a photo's content e.g. along an edge, near their personas. In an autograph book, Stan would sign first at the top or left hand side and Ollie immediately to the right or immediately parallel below, i.e. the autographs were together and not at different angles.

• Pitfalls. There are two main pitfalls; rubber stamps and pre-printed autographs. There are three or four different rubber stamps that were mostly applied by the Hal Roach film studios during the 1930s when Laurel and Hardy very popular and couldn't keep up the signing demands of the fan mail. Bright turquoise blue or black printers' ink was used. They can be quite deceptive to the eye and many top auction houses and UACC dealers have been caught out by them. However, the difference can be detected under a magnifying glass where the stamp shows breaks and unevenness in the ink and also presents a lack of flow that would be seen in a pen stroke. Pre-prints can also be difficult to detect if bought over the internet or bought under glass in a frame. Be aware that Stan 'officially' used a pre-print of their autographs after Ollie died in 1957. However Stan would countersign the photo in the bottom left corner and include an inscription in the middle which was often year dated (e.g. "63'). There are Laurel and Hardy autographs experts in the Laurel and Hardy Appreciation Society who are happy to give advice. (See Appendix II)'.

APPENDIX II

List of abbreviations, and helpful websites

THIS LIST SHOWS some abbreviations which you might encounter. (NB. Always check before purchasing, as the abbreviations may mean different things to different sellers. For instance, 'LS' could mean a letter written and signed by the same person, or it could mean the actual letter was written by someone else and just signed by the VIP.)

AD   Autograph Document (Hand-written)
ADS   Autograph Document Signed (Written and signed by the same person)
ALS   Autograph Letter Signed
AP   Autographed Photograph
AM   Autograph Manuscript (Hand-written music sheet, draft of play or novel.)
AN   Autographed Note
B&W   Black & White
DS   Document Signed
LS   Letter Signed
MS   Memo Signed or Manuscript
PS   Photograph Signed
SD   Signed Document,
SP   Signed Photograph
TLS   Typed Letter, Signed
TNS   Typed Note Signed

Useful information

AFTAL

The Autograph Fair Trade Association Limited (AFTAL) is a non-profit making body run for the benefit of its members and the general public, with a view to ensuring that the members can be relied upon to be trustworthy and duly qualified to perform their respective duties. AFTAL was created by a group of people who are directly involved in autographs, signed memorabilia and the organisation of related events. All decisions are made at board level, and all members are directly accountable to the board. Membership of the Association is an endorsement of the members' professional competence, and confirms to the public that the member is committed to providing authentic items, with all the required knowledge and diligence that that may demand. The organisation works together with the Police, Trading Standards, and Customs and Revenue officers to monitor and help stamp out the ever-growing problem of non-authentic signed memorabilia being sold and distributed throughout the UK.

Buckingham Covers

Buckingham Covers is based in Folkestone, Kent (South East England). It was founded in 2000 by two of the world's leading names in covers, Tony and Cath Buckingham. The covers are designed and made by the company and have grown enormously popularity - in most cases, doubling or tripling in price. It's a small company with a passion for covers, quality, customer service, charity fund raising and treating people decently. The company intends to make collecting fun every step of the way and to generate money for charities and good causes.

Fraser's

Fraser's are the UK market leaders who have been dealing in autographed material since 1978. They have provided thousands of customers all over the world with some of the finest collectables. The company understands that buying autographs can be a daunting task for even experienced collectors, so all its items are unconditionally guaranteed authentic for life. It is backed by Stanley Gibbons, the world's best-known name in collecting. Fraser's have a huge range of autographs on offer with over 60,000 items in stock spanning five centuries and including a unique range of photographs, historically important letters, documents, personal and film-worn clothing – all of which is constantly changing. Whether you are a serious investor or searching for an unusual gift, you will be purchasing a quality piece of history which will appeal to future generations and have investment potential. Fraser's gallery is at 399 The Strand, London.

MG Memorabilia

Although MG Memorabilia was created just a few years ago, the idea was there many years before. After visiting signing shows and enjoying the experience so much their hobby became a business. In line with similar companies, they are aware that the autograph industry has become full of people trying to make a fast buck by selling fake autographs, pre-prints and copies. MG Memorabilia aims to make sure that what customers buy is real and priced as competitively as possible. It is owned by Max Grenville and is a member of the UACC and AFTAL. MG Memorabilia: 4 Rosefield Court, Rosefield Street, Leamington Spa, Warwickshire, CV32 4HE.

Useful websites

AFTAL (Autograph Fair Trade Association Limited)
http://www.aftal.org.uk/

www.antiquedress.com
(Deborah Burke, seller of celebrity costume memorabilia)

Bonhams
http://www.bonhams.com/

Buckingham Covers
http://www.buckinghamcovers.co.uk/

www.carandclassic.co.uk

Fraser's
http://www.frasersautographs.com/

www.isitreal.com

www.laurelandhardy.org/autographs.html
(Or contact DTomlinson@tinyworld.co.uk for advice on collecting Laurel and Hardy autographs)

PADA (Professional Autograph Dealers Association)
www.padaweb.org

Library of Congress (Preserving Autographs)
http://www.loc.gov/preserv/careothr.html

UACC (The Universal Autograph Collectors Club Inc.)
http://www.uacc.org/

Recommended AFTAL dealers

Behind The Scenes: www.behindthescenes.org.uk
Montage Moments: www.montage-moments.com
Autografica: www.autografica.co.uk
Sport & Star Autographs: www.autographs.me.uk
Soccerbid: www.soccerbid.co.uk
Top Draw Memorabilia: www.TopDrawMemorabilia.co.uk
Autographs & Memorabilia: www.hertfordshireautographs.co.uk
Heroes & Legends: www.heroesandlegendsltd.co.uk
Memorabilia UK: www.memorabilia-uk.co.uk
Galaxy Collectables: www.galaxy-autographs.co.uk
Big Screen Collectables: www.bigscreenuk.com
Special Signings Limited: www.specialsignings.com
A Sign Of The Times Limited: www.asignofthetimeslimited.co.uk
Bid4sport Ltd: www.bid4sport.com
Memorabilia4U: www.memorabilia4u.com
MG Memorabilia: www.mgmemorabilia.co.uk
Colour of Sport Ltd: www.colourofsport.co.uk
Brandes Autographs: www.autogramme.com
Collectable Autographs: www.ddautographs.com
One Stop Autographs: www.hollywood-autographs.com
Stars & Icons: www.stars-icons.com
Autographs UK: www.autographs247.com

Further Reading

Assorted catalogues from auction houses, such as Fraser's
By Hook or By Crook: A Century of Autograph Thoughts, edited by
    Simon Goodenough, WI Books Ltd.
Collect Autographs: An Illustrated Guide to Collecting Autographs,
    (Various volumes) Stanley Gibbons Ltd.
Early Autograph Albums in the British Museum by M.A.E. Nickson,
    University Press, Oxford.

Acknowledgements

So many people lent me autograph books or sent in examples of rhymes, that it is impossible to mention them all. Special thanks, though, go to: Ellie Hopkins (Buckingham Covers), Claudia Cardoso (Fraser's), Olivia Odell (Fraser's), David Tomlinson (Laurel & Hardy Appreciation Society), Lorna Kaufman (Vectis), David Davies (AFTAL), Max Grenville (MG Memorabilia), Nik Askins, (H&H Group Holdings Limited), Jenna Brewer, Anne McAndrews, Sheri Munnich, Tracy Martin, Popps, Ruth Dale, Kathy Martin, Edith Smith, Trish Maunder, Deborah Burke.

I also would like to thank my long-suffering family – my husband Malcolm who spent hours photographing many of the autograph pages shown in this book, my son, Simon, who lent technical help and advice with some of the photos, and my daughter Jenna who ferried me to antique centres in my quest for autograph albums.

Photograph Credits

Nik Askins, H&H Group Holdings Ltd. 222 (top)
Behind the Scenes 142, 146
Malcolm Brewer 225
Simon Brewer 151
Buckingham covers 143, 151 (lower), 174, 175 (lower), 191, 195 (lower),
    199, 227 (lower), 228, 230, 231
Deborah Burke 214 (left)
Calebrw 198
Fraser's 145, 159, 160, 164, 173 (lower), 175, 183, 184, 187, 188, 189,
    190,194, 202, 207 (top), 210, 249, 251
Alan Light 147
Kathy Martin 196
Tracy Martin 209, 215
Trish Maunder 131
Peacay 14
J Picton 227
Matija Podwaski 242
MG Memorabilia 154, 155, 158
Notfromutrecht 224
Pearson Scott Foresman 245
Edith Smith 186
David Tomlinson 156, 157
Vectis 11, 165, 216, 217, 221(lower), 240

Other photographs are the property of the author.

Every effort has been made to ascertain the owner of the copyright of quotes,
rhymes and photographs used in this book.

Index of Album Quotes

269

General Index